THE CURE

Other books by Dave Bowler and Bryan Dray

U2: A Conspiracy of Hope
Genesis: A Biography

Dave Bowler
and **Bryan Dray**

the CURE

faith

PAN BOOKS

First published 1995 by Sidgwick & Jackson

This edition published 1996 by Pan Books
an imprint of Macmillan General Books
25 Eccleston Place, London SW1W 9NF
and Basingstoke

Associated companies throughout the world

ISBN 0 330 34692 X

9 8 7 6 5 4 3 2 1

A CIP catalogue record for this book is available from
the British Library

Typeset by CentraCet Limited, Cambridge
Printed and bound in Great Britain by
Cox & Wyman Ltd, Reading, Berkshire

To Mom and Dad
For making all things possible
And for Denise
God's answer to Job.
Always
DAVID

Friends make the difference, especially
Jane and Larry, Simon and Marissa, Tony and Nancy,
Eric Medcraft and Jo Gaiter. And as ever
Trish, Emma and Rebecca
for their love and support.
And Mum, Dad, Gran, Joyce and Wal
without whom . . .
BRYAN

Contents

Acknowledgements

THERE ARE any number of people who have been of help in the preparation of this book. In particular, we would like to thank Tim Pope and Lisa Bryer for their time and trouble in helping to arrange and conduct Tim's interview. For all aspiring journalists out there, let it be known there are few more entertaining interviewees.

The music press has again been of invaluable assistance in the course of the book's basic research and we'd like to express our thanks to the staff and contributors at *Melody Maker*, *New Musical Express*, *Sounds*, *Q*, *Vox*, *Zig Zag*, *Lime Lizard*, *Select*, *Blitz*, *Keyboard*, *International Musician & Recording World*, *RCD*, *Record Collector* and *The Times* for their gracious permission to reprint from their work – a full list of sources can be found elsewhere in the book.

We also have to thank Fiction Records and all those at Sidgwick & Jackson who have helped with the project since its inception. We are especially grateful to Tanja, Charlotte and Jessica at the Tanja Howarth Literary Agency for large quantities of advice – and, more importantly, sympathy – at crucial times during the writing of the manuscript.

It doesn't matter how great you think the Cure are, when you're writing about them, there comes a point when you can't face listening to 'One Hundred Years' for the twenty-fifth time that day. For refreshing the critical faculties at such vital moments, eternal thanks go to Lush and Kristin Hersh for providing 1994's finest moments to date. We are therefore indebted to Colleen at 4AD's press office.

Finally, to our families. Again we are very grateful for your support throughout the whole process of writing and researching this tome. Without Denise's selfless decision to go on holiday for a couple of weeks, this book might never have been finished . . .

This book was written on an IBM PS/1 using Microsoft Works software. Does this mean we get a sponsorship deal now?

Authors' Note

THE purpose of this book is to take a detached, objective view of the Cure's work. It is not designed to be Robert Smith's own story – for that you should look elsewhere. It is an attempt to make sense of what has at times been a very complicated tale and to shed light on the reasons why the Cure, and more especially Smith, have taken the decisions that they have and what repercussions followed.

As perhaps the only stadium band in the world that have been able to maintain critical credibility over a sustained period, the Cure are in a unique position. Just how that enviable status has been achieved is the central theme of this book.

Introduction

SURPRISING as it may seem, Robert Smith, lead singer and driving force behind the Cure, has now reached the status of bona fide 'superstar'. Although when he first appeared in the pages of the music press in the late seventies it was clear that here might be another rock icon in the making, a figure upon whom many myths and legends might ultimately be centred, it always seemed likely that Smith and the Cure would achieve that status within a relatively small circle of admirers and passionate devotees rather than being feted by mainstream culture as a purveyor of perfect pop. Bets were taken that he would become a punk Frank Zappa rather than an existential Paul McCartney. That Smith and his crew have been able to straddle the fine line between commercial success and critical credibility makes them almost unique at present and represents a long and intriguing journey from their first faltering musical efforts almost twenty years ago.

For a band that does not have so much a family tree as a family orchard, so regular have been the changes in line-up and personnel, there has remained just one constant factor; Robert Smith. Inevitably the evolution of the Cure is inextricably linked with that of Smith. He has changed in outlook over the years, as the numerous musical styles which the Cure have explored demonstrate, but the cartoon shorthand of folklore has the Cure as either doomy goths hanging upside down in assorted belfries plying their stock-in-trade miserable anthems or, just as misleading, skittish coquettes indulging in squirming, treacly pop. Smith is a far more complex and original musician than that simplistic view would credit and has moved through various phases of inspiration and yet, with very few exceptions, he has remained faithful to the original motivation that brought the band to life. In this fashion he has carried through his initial intensity of purpose.

As undisputed leader of the Cure, his approach to band mates has been similarly volatile. Originally little more than one of the group at the time of their first recordings, Smith became more and more the focal point on and off stage and began to dominate the direction of the group, its aims, its personnel and its approach. By the time of *Pornography*, the fourth album released in 1982, Smith and the Cure had become virtually synonymous. The ferocious tenacity with which he clung to his original vision was often misunderstood, though his self-confessed penchant for obnoxious behaviour around the time did little to endear him to commentators. As a consequence, he and the Cure became solely identified with a funereal style of music. Since the peripheral political games of the music industry were of no interest to Smith he found himself adrift with few allies, heading towards a future as a bit player marooned on the fringes. More worryingly, Smith increasingly had the mantle of Ian Curtis of Joy Division foisted upon him, the next introspective rock star ready to die for his audience. All of this conspired to drive the Cure further and further down a blind alley from which there seemed no escape as commercial success eluded them – a situation which, perversely, Smith seemed to relish – and even the core of fans and journalists who had supported the Cure began to lose faith in the group and their prospects.

At their nadir they were barely tolerated by the music industry; now the Cure are feted by the industry moguls, and several labels have tried to entice them away from Polydor through whom Fiction's outpourings are distributed. Smith has fashioned a future for the original nihilistic punk message. Once punk had destroyed the old order its standard bearers were burned out, astounded by their success and with no new concrete ideas to put in place, hence their almost immediate demise. In contrast, the Cure, a group whom Smith still tags as 'vaguely punk', were steadfast in their ideas, possessing what George Bush poetically termed 'the vision thing' in bucketfuls. True to the DIY punk philosophy, Smith has retained control over his career at every level and has been able to exert his influence on every step the group have taken. The Cure have illustrated that a group which has been around a long time can play a stadium with style rather than bluster, that a highly successful band need not be careerist, and that a group does not have to sell its artistic soul to achieve commercial success. Smith has always done just what he chooses and it is that attitude as much as the music that has gradually uncovered a like-minded constituency across the globe, turning each new Cure project into a real event for fans and accountants alike.

How did that turn-round happen? Faith has been a key principle in the story of the Cure, with Smith keeping the band together when things might easily have gone awry. That singlemindedness which saw them through the first phase of their career has worked to their advantage as they have developed a wider audience with their dogged refusal to engage in publicity stunts that would compromise their music and approach. From a band that began life with an 'anti-image', they have grown to the point where for many buying a Cure record is far more than simply getting a collection of songs but is effectively a point of embarkation, the focus of a far wider package that embraces an entire ethos spearheaded by a group that has its own rules, its own guide-lines and which chooses to do things in its own time, in its own way. In so doing, in creating a real and effective unorthodoxy, Smith and the Cure have regularly missed opportunities to sell a lot of records very quickly but have, in maintaining their original ideals, developed a devoted audience with whom a real bond exists. Few artists have combined longevity, critical credibility and commerciality to such great effect.

It is ironic therefore that the second phase of the Cure's evolution and the seeds of their greater acceptance were sown in the form of compromise when, in the aftermath of *Pornography*, Smith chose to release three of the most blatant slices of pop that he has ever recorded in an attempt to free himself from the baggage that the previous four albums had generated. Smith's recognition of the problems that threatened the band was evident in his choice of output and the restructuring of the Cure to a core of himself and co-founder Lol Tolhurst. So entrenched had their non-personalities become in the public mind that further surgery was clearly required to change wider opinion and so Smith wrote 'Let's Go To Bed', 'The Walk' and 'The Lovecats', musical attempts to shed light on the humour, albeit bleak, that already existed in the group but which rarely came across – clearly anyone who is able to call a song 'The Funeral Party' either has his tongue in his cheek or his head up his backside and public opinion tended to favour the latter. To take the development one stage further, it was time that the Cure mastered the promotional video, something they had singularly failed to do; 'Charlotte Sometimes' remains the most leaden, depressing example of the genre ever unleashed on an unsuspecting public. Yet it was this medium that perhaps played the most striking part in taking the Cure on to a different plane as they became involved in a long-standing partnership with video director extraordinaire Tim Pope.

The quirky, amusing and seemingly out of character films that Smith, Tolhurst and Pope put together for those three singles represented not merely the beginning of the band's rise to a position of greater commercial clout but the start of a further period of evolution in their internal democracy. Smith had taken over the reins to such an extent that the Cure was running the risk of becoming a dictatorship but the success of his collaboration with Pope reawakened him to the potential that might be tapped in other areas of the group's existence.

Tim Pope was the first person that Robert Smith came to treat as an artistic equal. This changed Smith's perspective and, over a period of years, the Cure transformed itself from a benign dictatorship where input from others was sometimes encouraged but wasn't always used to a quasi-democratic unit where everyone was given a far more equal role to play. A different writing regime evolved where the input of other people became more valued and valuable – though Smith remains first among equals – and this has inevitably produced different musical directions which have widened their appeal. Almost as important have been the promotional films they've made and which are awaited with almost the same degree of anticipation as the new songs. These played a crucial role in their development from an introspective unit whose cult status was assured but who never really threatened greater things, to artists who were able to very successfully cross over into the mainstream without compromising their music in any way. That is not to say that Pope is the reason for the Cure's success, for without the songs he would have nothing to do, but it is true that he, in tandem with Smith and, to a lesser extent, the other members of the group, has been able to fashion a visual representation of the band that has made it far easier for them to cut through to the less committed music buyer, those who make the difference between gold and platinum status.

This was clearly illustrated by the British Phonographic Industry's annual jamboree and back-slapping on-expenses booze-up – or the Brit Awards to give it its appropriately tatty but better known moniker. Historically the awards are a desert of disappointment for anyone who might have any hope for the future health of British music. Quite apart from the amateurish staging year after year, this ritual reaches its real nadir with the distribution of its gongs. Rarely do the votes extend beyond the predictable magic circle of artists such as Dire Straits, Simply Red, Eric Clapton and Elton John – and this in the best female vocalist category. Depending upon your level of commitment to British popular music, you may find this boring but inevitable as the awards become little more than an extension of the album charts or you may find it a betrayal of everything that made Britain the epicentre of the rock world in the 1960s – its eccentricity, its humour, its passion, its idiosyncrasies and its over-whelming refusal to take itself too seriously. As the bloated and the pompous repeat last year's acceptance speeches and the watching millions anxiously await the glorious finale featuring Mark Knopfler and his all-star band, countless others switch off and wonder why there wasn't anything new on offer.

In a blinding flash of lucidity just prior to a liquid lunch, the democratic process for the 1989 awards somehow allowed the Cure, a group that embodies so many of those archetypal qualities, to slip through the net and actually win a cateogry. It was especially apposite that they won the Best Video prize since they more than most have exploited that medium's possibilities artistically and in so doing have generated great commercial success as distinct from those who have embraced it purely as a marketing tool. More significantly, at the following year's show they carried away the Best British Group silverware. Though Smith and company – along with their fans – will have remained stoically unimpressed by this supposedly presti-gious accolade, it did finally confirm that the Cure were a vital component of the British recording industry from whom great things were expected, and represented a staging point in their idiosyncratic evolution. That evolution forms the central core of this book: the relationships, the shifts in emphasis and presentation and the way in which the Cure ultimately survived and then went on to succeed when all conventional wisdom suggested they would fall. The Cure story is a story of faith.

Chapter One

'**D**ISINTEGRATION was a brilliant period, it was brilliant to do something with that kind of intensity, but you can't stay like that. We all got in quite a state again by the end of the American leg of the tour, the concerts were really fierce, the whole thing was manic. The last nights in Boston I thought, "Aah, I'm here, this is what I've always wanted," but everything just went to pieces after that on a lot of levels with the group, as it always does, you can't maintain it. Frustration sets in and everything becomes so commonplace.'

With these words Smith encapsulated the essence of the Cure – a shambolic lurching creature that is sometimes beyond the absolute control even of its master Robert Smith but which at the height of its powers is able to drown those who surround it in wave after wave of mesmerizing emotion. It is that fragility, that very human inconsistency which forms the core of the band, its transient nature which fuels Smith's creative instincts. His confession that 'if I didn't feel the Cure could fall apart at any minute it would be completely worthless' is a statement symptomatic of his refusal to allow the group's position to become set in stone and the band to degenerate into some lumpen dinosaur supergroup, but also one which recognizes that that very frailty and the prospect of their impending demise spurs them onwards.

It's an attitude of mind that is empathic with the punk zeitgeist which prevailed at the time of the band's earliest professional work but one to which the Cure have remained far more faithful than most of their contemporaries. The regular changes in personnel have conspired to provide useful injections of fresh ideas and personalities while Smith is far harder on himself and the rest of the band, particularly in writing terms, than almost any other artist you could care to name. The reputation the Cure have constructed is clearly precious to him and he refuses to cash in on the fact that the Cure will 'shift units' on the back of their name alone, ensuring that anything he considers sub-standard will not see the light of day. His voice remains the one that calls the shots.

Robert hasn't always been quite so obviously the ringmaster of the Cure circus, however. As has been the case with many groups right down the rock 'n' roll age, the band took its formative steps in the classroom – or, to be more accurate, to avoid the classroom. The group began in Crawley, where Robert and co-founder Laurence Tolhurst first encountered one another on a school bus in September 1964 when both were five, though it was not until 1972 that they found themselves thrown together along with the other early Cure, Michael Dempsey, and were able to strike up a friendship based around shared musical tastes. Smith, born in April 1959, already stuck out from the crowd by virtue of a pronounced northern accent. His parents Alex and Rita had moved south from their Blackpool home when he was three, along with the rest of the family which comprised a brother and sister a decade older than him and his infant sister. Perhaps as a consequence of being saddled with that most anonymous of surnames, Smith has always striven to be an individual, a leader rather than a follower.

If his early schooling was fairly unremarkable at St Francis Primary and Junior school, it was the move to the Notre Dame Middle School in 1970 that first provided Smith with the opportunity to express himself musically. He had been playing guitar since the age of six, taking formal lessons, against which he quickly rebelled after Christmas 1972 when he received his first guitar as a present. Growing from the roots of social change in the sixties, Notre Dame was the guinea pig for an educational experiment, allowing pupils artistic and intellectual freedom rather than simply inculcating the 'Three Rs'. It was at this school that Robert really got to know Lol Tolhurst, two months Robert's senior, and embarked on the road that was to lead to the Cure's formation. The school's approach was so very different to the norm that it had a more profound effect on the group than merely being the venue where they began making music.

Smith has tended to speak in disparaging, faintly patronizing terms about the school and its ideals. He avers that he went to school wearing a black velvet dress simply to test out the teachers' reactions, recalling that 'my teachers were so liberal they tried hard not to notice', thinking that he was going through a personality crisis. However, no contemporaries can recall this particular incident and so it may be an early example of Smith's penchant for what might kindly be described as talking in parables or, perhaps more accurately, lying through his teeth for the sake of a good story. This is the man who hoodwinked the press into believing he took a sheep on tour with him, after all. Fact or fiction, the point is that Robert affects great distaste for that particular regime, possibly because it was so difficult for him to shock or rebel against its authority figures, figures for whom in general he retains a healthy disregard.

Nevertheless, the freedom of thought and the artistic bent of its teaching must have proved inspirational to Smith and has had a lasting effect on his approach to his work. Suggesting that someone who has sold in excess of 20 million records works purely on the principle of art for art's sake is a little far-fetched, for that level of success demands a keen business brain that can spot opportunities for his music but Smith seemingly retains a greater feeling for his art than do many others of his ilk who have been willing to compromise their artistic ideals in order to sell more records. At this point in time, Smith need never work again such is his financial security but it is still the idea of creating music that spurs him on – his early exposure at Notre Dame to the idea of art being as important as arithmetic clearly helped in shaping that philosophy.

While Smith would find the comparisons appalling, it's instructive to remember that a few years later in Dublin, the members of U2 found themselves thrown together in a highly unconventional educational environment – a non-denominational school, the first such in Ireland, with a leaning towards the arts. That background drew talents from those individuals that might not have come to light at another school and it's reasonable to suggest that Notre Dame can, in the Cure's success, claim a similar vindication of its methods.

It is perhaps understandable that the school is loath to acknowledge Smith's existence in the light of his occasional sniping at the establishment but nevertheless it played a crucial role in setting the group on their way, providing a music rehearsal facility which Smith, Tolhurst and Dempsey put to use as an escape route from the rigours of religious and other education. Robert has suggested that the teachers' acceptance of this educational trade-off came about simply because of his advanced ability to kid them that here was a 'special' talent when in fact he was simply trying to avoid the more tedious timetable of regular education but this seems harsh. Rather than appearing gullible, in hindsight the staff seem to have been remarkably prescient in recognizing his abilities and providing him with a springboard for his later success. Although there is general agreement that the music they made while at Notre Dame was less than impressive, they were given the time and opportunity to learn their instruments and develop a musical approach which stood them in good stead when they began to play on a professional basis years later. Smith was just nineteen when their first album was recorded and most of the songs had been written when he was even younger, a remarkably precocious performance that can only have been helped by the chances given to him at this middle school.

Notre Dame's success with regard to Smith is ironically most marked in his rejection of the school's ideas and teaching: the very spirit of self-sufficient, individualistic thinking that they wanted to encourage in their pupils is very obvious in his character. It's entirely in keeping with his self-contained attitude to himself and his music, a stubborn refusal to admit the value of any outside influences and a desire to go about things in his own way and in his own time. Only someone fiercely independent in spirit could have followed the often wilfully uncommercial path that he has through his musical career and while such a spirit is perhaps a natural trait it was very evidently encouraged by the relatively freewheeling attitude of Notre Dame. The only musical concession the proto-Cure appear to have had to make to the school is to invent a covering religious pretext for their music, incorporating random religious phraseology into their lyrics.

The school did have natural material from which to work, however. Robert's elder brother, Richard, thirteen years his senior, had already perpetrated all the usual adolescent 'crimes' that drive parents mad the world over and so Robert had a fairly relaxed childhood. Interestingly, Lol's family background was fairly similar; he was the fifth of six children, the fourth boy, with a gap of eight years between him and his elder sister Jane. Robert's father's attitude to life and work was clearly an inspiration to Robert, who remarked to *Melody Maker* that he 'jacked in his job 'cos it made him unhappy and he didn't want to compromise his entire life just for the sake of carrying it through. It's very admirable, that quality . . . you have to refuse to give in.' The father's determination to live life according to his own values was to be found in abundance in the son. As an extension of that philosophy it is easy to understand just why he now claims to have found the whole Notre Dame experience worthless since it was a period where he was not in sole control of his own life, control being probably the central theme of Smith's work and existence. Everything that he has done in setting up and then running the Cure has been designed to engineer for himself a separate existence away from the mundanities of ordinary life.

While Smith was clearly a precocious child, it is unlikely that his early musical experiments with Tolhurst and Dempsey and other class mates Alan Hill and Marc Ceccagno were anything other than simple fun and an escape from the school curriculum rather than the beginnings of a masterplan for his career. While at Notre Dame, this new group, who called themselves the Obelisk, played a concert for their class which was, by Smith's own account, horrible, but most interestingly it featured Dempsey and Ceccagno as guitarists and him on piano as very much a background player. Viewed in the light of his dominant personality in later years, it is almost inconceivable to imagine Robert Smith not leading the group. Michael Dempsey recalls meeting Lol well before Robert, noting that Lol was the memorable personality while Robert was a more peripheral character who took time to come to the fore, partly the result of his habit of withdrawing into himself. Michael was the oldest of the three core Cures, having first seen the light of day in November 1958 in what was then Salisbury, Rhodesia, and is now Harare, Zimbabwe. His parents, William and Nancy, moved the family of Michael, his elder sister Anne and baby brother Martin to England in 1961, Michael eventually finding his way to Notre Dame at the same time as Lol and Robert.

Playing as the Obelisk was one of the final acts of their tenure at Notre Dame, before they moved on at thirteen to St Wilfrid's secondary school to complete their education. What effect did Notre Dame have on Robert Smith? Most noticeably it appears to have bolstered his confidence, suggesting that idiosyncrasy and an individual style of thought could be valid in modern society, a central theme of the Cure's work later. Robert confessed that, 'To lose the idea of verse/chorus/middle eight/chorus/end in a song . . . is really import-ant to us,' a clear rejection of the prevailing format of a century of popular music. Notre Dame also gave him the opportunity to play music within a group format in a contemporary style as opposed to the choral and classical tradition that so many schools impose on those children expressing an interest in music. In addition, it allowed him to get through two years of schooling with the minimum of religious education and so the move to St Wilfrid's with its strict Roman Catholic teaching was clearly something of a culture shock.

Smith was brought up in a Catholic household but regular churchgoing was not a ritual which his parents imposed on their children and Robert was quick to excuse himself from devotional duties, initially because there were more interesting and entertaining ways of passing the time than dredging through drab liturgy. Having to revert to a Catholic education at the age of thirteen wasn't something to which he took kindly, finally getting expelled at one point along with Marc Ceccagno because of his undesirable attitude, before the school allowed him back to complete his exams. The nucleus of Smith, Tolhurst, Dempsey and Ceccagno all moved to the new school together and it was as a reaction to enforced discipline that the new academic hierarchy foisted upon them that they began to formalize their music, creating their own personal environment in opposition to that which controlled their working hours. It wasn't until January 1976, however, that they had their first serious rehearsal although a constantly varying line-up had played on an ad hoc basis in the extension of Robert's parents' home in Crawley. This putative Cure found themselves unable to play other people's songs because of their initial musical deficiencies and so were experimenting with developing their own sound, though Dempsey has suggested that, in common with the Stranglers' line, there were no heroes for them to emulate and they were determined simply to provide an alternative. By this point Robert had taken centre stage on guitar with Michael moving to bass and Lol usurping an early and largely unremembered incumbent of the drum stool, Graham, who left when Robert sacked his brother, the lead vocalist. Lol quickly became the only contender for the vacancy when Michael persuaded him of the wisdom of investing in a drum kit.

The church hall might have seemed an odd location in some respects for Robert to spend his time given his lack of interest in religion but the hall was made available to the group and they were in no position to look a gift horse in the mouth. The group, using the gruesome epithet Malice, now consisted of Smith, Dempsey, Tolhurst and Ceccagno and between them they discovered an added attraction in their rehearsal space. 'The line-up used to fluctuate between five and fifteen,' recalls Smith. 'In the hall, there was a bar and with a long piece of bamboo cane you could reach through the grille to the optics. Then you could get at the drink and so we could all get completely mortal.' This interest in what Robert is pleased to call 'social drinking' has been an enduring source of Cure stories, some probably apocryphal, others not, but it is true to say that, even at this early stage, the group's social life was assuming at least an equal importance to the music they were making.

In the summer of 1975, the individuals in the band had taken their 'O' levels and were coming ever closer to having to make career decisions and to going out into the world beyond the cloistered confines of academia, so it is significant that Malice embarked on more serious rehearsals in 1976. Dempsey and Smith chose to prolong their education at St Wilfrid's, attending sixth form there, both studying English Literature, Robert also taking French at 'A' level, while Lol Tolhurst moved to technical college in Crawley where he studied chemistry.

Of them all, Robert felt most keenly the need to make contingency plans in order to avoid the conventional path of university and responsible job, a future to which he was vehemently opposed. He later admitted, 'I'd never work. If life became a series of alarm calls and unendurable days I'd very seriously question [committing suicide],' adding, 'the reason we formed this band wasn't for all the usual reasons like being bored. It was so we didn't have to get up at nine in the morning, so we didn't have to work for other people.' Faced with the creeping inevitability of that kind of life, Smith in particular chose to take a more positive interest in Malice, though his infatuation with the Sensational Alex Harvey Band acted as an equally important catalyst.

Smith spent a year following them around the country in the company of his girlfriend, Mary Poole, whom he had met at St Wilfrid's during a drama class when he was fourteen and who was to quickly become the mainstay of his life. The Sensational Alex Harvey Band were something of an oddity on the music scene in the mid-seventies, having some empathy with the glam rock boom while playing a harder-edged style of music adapted and mutated from the blues. It was in terms of their presentation that they were truly original, however, creating a form of rock theatre into which devotees could completely escape for the duration of a show. The influence of the SAHB's theatricality wasn't obvious in the Cure's work but there were subtle nods in their direction in the way in which the Cure were to attempt to make their concerts all-encompassing events.

In 1976, however, all of this was a long way off as Malice struggled through their repertoire of songs and odd cover versions. They rehearsed fairly intensively until Marc Ceccagno became a casualty, leaving to start a jazz rock outfit called Amulet. By the autumn, he had been replaced by local guitar hero Porl Thompson, the only member of the troupe to have a day job, working as a waiter at Gatwick airport. Thompson was born in Wimbledon in November 1957, and spent two years in Australia as an infant before he and his two brothers and older sister returned with parents Tom and Dot to Crawley in 1964. He had met Smith in a record shop where they discovered they shared similar tastes though Thompson's playing style was more aggressive. He was also able to bring a far greater level of musical ability and technique into the band. Two years senior to the others, his presence called their work into question and Smith in particular was forced to reassess his own playing and role within the band, a necessary period of questioning which provided the impetus to kick start his own songwriting. Tapes of the band from around this period suggest that they dabbled with a fairly belligerent approach that bordered on hard rock at times, although so haphazard was their work, it's difficult to discern any common thread. There were hints of other artists in their playing, particularly SAHB, Bowie and Hendrix while more unlikely influences included Captain Beefheart.

'In 1976, we had about 100 rehearsals and knew six songs,' Robert noted, 'so we thought we'd do it in public. The first gig was in the school – I convinced the head that we should have a Christmas concert with a jazz ensemble; that was us! The curtain opened and we were there, snarling. It was a disaster. I started with a different song and was one ahead all the way through without noticing until they started the last song and I'd already played it.'

Other recollections are, perhaps inevitably, rather different. The school show was actually their second performance in a week, the first coming at Worth Abbey where they had engineered a booking by pretending to be a folk band, requiring them to play an acoustic set in what was an uncannily farsighted rehearsal for their MTV Unplugged session fifteen years later. Or it may just have been a coincidence. The school show saw them supporting Marc Ceccagno's Amulet and featured a local journalist as singer. The show which sounded like nothing other than thirty minutes of feedback culmi-nated in their new lead singer quitting on the spot, the concert collapsing into riot as the few audience members remaining took to the stage.

It's instructive to remember that Robert was in no way the undisputed leader of the group – he wasn't the singer at this point and nor was he the only songwriter. Lol had one particular piece around at the time called 'Easy Cure'. After the débâcle of the Christmas concert, no one had any sentimental attachment to the name Malice and so the newly constituted nucleus of Smith, Thompson, Tolhurst and Dempsey began to trade under the moniker the Easy Cure, convening regularly again at Robert's house throughout the early months of 1977 and running through a further two vocalists who failed to make the grade and were unable to fit into the already tight-knit Easy Cure community. Throughout this period, both the music and the musicians were undergoing a period of transition, influenced by musical developments beyond the cosy confines of Crawley.

Punk had started to scrawl its signature across the national psyche, most notably of course in the shape of the Sex Pistols, but they were far from being the only band involved. To a group of youngsters isolated from the London clubs where much of this sea-change was taking place, the musical message was transmitted largely by John Peel's late-night show on Radio 1 as, over a period of about eighteen months, his staple output went from prog-rock to punk-rock. Robert was a seasoned Peel veteran by 1977, having become a regular listener some three years earlier, but the effect of hearing the Buzzcocks or the Clash was every bit as pivotal in his life as his early encounters with Alex Harvey had been. The Easy Cure did not change their style or direction overnight and they never became a punk band in any sense that the media would recognize but the external events of 1977 were nevertheless crucial to their development.

If punk did nothing else, and from a distance of two decades its legacy seems increasingly insubstantial, an incoherent rant that changed little, it can claim some credit for the birth of the independent recording sector which wrenched some artistic and financial control from the major labels, turning the spotlight back onto the artists and their primary function to entertain and, hopefully, engage their audience intellectually not with incomprehensible cosmic waffle but with acerbic comments on ordinary life. To a degree, punk removed the barriers between audience and artist with its philosophy that anyone with a point to make could make it musically whether they were able to handle an instrument or not. The Easy Cure felt that they did have something to say and that the music business was gradually coming round to their way of thinking.

To attach to punk the gravitas that innumerable portentous commentaries have since bestowed upon it is to miss the real point. Punk never was a political phenomenon in the way that Malcolm McLaren might try to describe it, it was not a neo-Nazi movement despite the liberal use of Nazi symbolism and paraphernalia and nor was it the end of civilization as we knew it. For those who were its adherents at the time, before the music press seized it and turned it into their personal property, punk was a good laugh, a source of some mindless fun, enjoyment wrenched from a depressing country then going through an unpleasant phase of Establishment-led patriotism surrounding the Queen's Silver Jubilee.

Punk was largely a London-led movement in its infancy, though to be strictly accurate it was not the city of London but the outlying districts and the satellite towns of suburbia where it took hold. Those that began punk were those who were denied access to the glitz and glamour of London's nightlife by economic or geographic consider-ations and who, on the infrequent occasions they did pierce its armour, were left stoically unimpressed by a capital that loved itself yet seemed to offer nothing to bored teenagers unaffected by its garishly ostentatious display of a wealth to which they were not given access. One of the most visible and renowned of such groupings was known as the Bromley Contingent, which included Susan Dallion, later to gain fame as Siouxsie Sioux, and Steve Severin with whom she was to form Siouxsie and the Banshees. Unlike their contempor-aries in other parts of the country, these kids had the chance to see what was on offer but no opportunity to participate, a rubbing of salt into the open wounds of adolescent tristesse. Simply, the prototype punks made their own entertainment because they had to and because they wanted to and it was not until later that it took on its own manifesto allowing in more people with wider ranging, sometimes very different, motivations. Its original inspiration was as a means of escape, Severin pointing out in John Lydon's autobiography *Rotten* that 'by definition and out of need, we were into making our own fun'.

The need for escapism felt by a frustrated crop of teenagers had inevitable consequences. Punk wasn't going to be forced into a corner and so it came out fighting, all guns blazing, giving punk its leering aggression, the aggression of the cornered animal. The punk movement quickly grew from fun into something different as the resentment that individuals like Johnny Rotten felt found its way into the music – a rage against the powers that be that sought to relegate them to the status of factory fodder or dole queuers. To capture the moment, the music had to be made fast and since punk was in some ways a celebration of the resilience of the spirit against towering odds, by definition it had to be primitive – if you had had instruments and music lessons provided for you, what did you have to be angry about? The first punk wave seized whatever instruments they could, plugged in and made their noise, the joining point for many who had been on the outside. Articulating their own emotions was important, not musical proficiency, and as a defence mechanism they poured scorn on those that had gone before them, the dinosaurs of rock who had betrayed their original talents and were surviving solely on technical ability – plastic soul.

The Easy Cure could understand the frustration of suburban youth since they were just as tantalizingly close to the alleged excitement of the bright lights without access to them but it was the principles and ideas behind this new music that excited them rather than those behind the movement. As a band, they were limited as far as technique went but they had ideas, things to say, points to make as well as a desire to enjoy themselves. Under the conventional wisdom that held before 1976, the Easy Cure would have had to spend years rehearsing and honing their instrumental skills before they might dare to venture on to vinyl but punk shattered that particular piece of folly. For a brief period before the Establishment, in the shape of the press and the record companies, moved in to homogenize and sanitize it all, there were no more heroes and no more rules, as Severin pointed out. 'This musical era [didn't] represent a musical crusade. It was more like you're given this opportunity . . . it was a time that manifested itself. You couldn't dream of the same opportunity coming along again.' That brief period stimulated the Easy Cure and allowed them to slip through the net. The return to the roots of pure power pop inspired the Peel-guzzling Smith who later recalled hearing the Only Ones' 'Another Girl Another Planet' from one of those sessions in April 1978 and 'I just thought "this is what I want to do"'.

Smith the individual was developing rapidly at this period and the invigorating times in which he was fortunate enough to live provided further impetus. As the group progressed through 1977 it became increasingly obvious that there was the potential for this to become more than just a fun way of passing the time. Michael dropped out of school and was working as a hospital porter while Lol was combining his studies with work experience in industrial chemistry. For Robert, school was coming to a close, he had no desire to prolong his education further and he certainly had no intention of going to work, so the time had again come to take the Easy Cure a step further. With the addition of yet another new vocalist, Peter O'Toole, they were ready to embark on their first foray into the world beyond Crawley.

Chapter Two

PROBABLY the biggest, most daunting step which any new group has to make is the one which takes them beyond the cosy confines of their own neighbourhood where they can perform to those who know them well and who are likely to be as caught up in the excitement and novelty inspired by a local act as the group themselves. To discover whether or not your group has talents which the rest of the world may find appealing, you have to go out into that world and make yourself known. The traditional method in rock circles is to go on the road and play your songs the length and breadth of the country, hopefully constructing a core audience and garnering some press attention on the way. Given their idiosyncratic style and personality, it was perhaps inevitable that the Easy Cure did not initially choose this well-worn route though eventually it was one they had to follow.

Robert Smith in particular was a self-sufficient teenager confident of the music that he and the group were writing and playing. Indeed since their early sound came together through rejection of what had gone before rather than by emulation of early heroes, the very premise of the Easy Cure was that they *had* to be better than anyone else. Dempsey told *Record Collector* with just a hint of exaggeration, 'We were dismissive of virtually everything and that was the way we developed our sound . . . we weren't eclectic. Rather than put together all the bits in pop we really liked we did it the other way round. We took away all the bits we didn't like.' The group were in sympathy with the punk cause of sweeping away all that had gone before but contemptuous of its inability to replace it with anything more interesting. The Easy Cure approached punk with a healthy dose of cynicism, recognizing that many of those involved were simply out for the same rewards that the previous generation, the very people they were attacking, had won for themselves.

The confidence that the Easy Cure had in themselves was striking from a band who had done so little to justify it thus far – after all, aside from their rehearsals they had merely played a handful of decidedly unimpressive concerts in their locale. Some of this assurance, arrogance even, can again be ascribed to their schooling, particularly at Notre Dame where unconventional ideas had been encouraged in varying degrees and so concepts that might have appeared offbeat or artistically precious to others did not strike them as extreme. The attitude of the group was simply to reject external opinion since their personal experience taught them that 'art' was a wholly valid area in which to be involved and was not synonymous with the overblown pomposity that had characterized the 'art-rock' of the preceding years. Being scornful of almost any other musicians you might care to name, the Easy Cure were content in the sure knowledge that they were more interesting and worthwhile than any competition there might be. If others caught on, then so much the better.

Having progressed to the point at which they had a clutch of self-penned songs in hand, the group were indulging in that traditional young musicians' pastime of scrutinizing the music press. In April of 1977, they came across an advert in *Melody Maker* placed by Hansa Records, the self-proclaimed leading pop record label in Germany. Beneath the headline 'Wanna be a recording star?' and the timeless catch phrase 'get your ass up – take your chances!' was a spiel appealing for groups and singers to send tapes and photos to the company so that they might be auditioned. Manfully ignoring the appalling advertising copy, the artless photography featuring a glitter-clad groupie and the small print testament that Hansa were in fact the people responsible for the success of Donna Summer and Boney M, the Easy Cure decided that this was the break for which they'd been patiently waiting and put together a tape at Robert's house. Within days, Robert received a telegram asking him to call the company as soon as possible in order to arrange an audition.

The idea of record companies advertising in the music press for new talent was not a new one nor has it died out, as a cursory glance at the classified pages of *Melody Maker* or *New Musical Express* proves. None the less the very idea has its seamier side and such adverts are often placed by exploitative management or recording companies looking to make a quick buck. That Hansa were not of that ilk was particularly fortuitous for a young and very naive band.

There again, if Hansa, part of the Ariola group, refused to take advantage of the innocence displayed by the Easy Cure in financial terms, they clearly had very different views on the band's future. Such management adverts are generally placed by companies looking for youthful charges either as a package or with a view to plucking individuals from different outfits before moulding them into one group with which to take on the world. Teenage groups have long been assembled in this manner right from the earliest days of pop music through groups such as the Monkees right up to the point at which the Hansa advert appeared, with a rush of 1970s groups long since consigned to the dustbin of pop trivia – groups such as Flintlock or Child, for instance. In Europe there was seen to be little, if anything, wrong with this approach as Hansa's involvement with the likes of Boney M indicated. The Eurodisco milieu was filled with such Frankenstein creations and so with hindsight their advertising campaign makes greater sense, saving on the onerous and expensive leg work that an A&R department would be otherwise forced to undertake.

Naturally, the Easy Cure had no such understanding of this side of the deal. To them, a record company was a record company which must always be on the look-out for new talent. Their original assumption was simply that their punk-tinged power-pop had caught the attention of an organization looking to dip its toes into these new musical waters and so they were only too delighted to respond quickly to the telegram, leading to a video audition to be held in London's Morgan Studios on 13 May. Playing a couple of their own songs, the group were filmed by Hansa's representatives in the course of a session which quickly deteriorated into farce, as Robert recalled: 'We did a video for them of us performing and I don't think they were listening. I remember my guitar strap broke in the middle of the song and the guitar fell on the floor. I was standing there looking at the control room and the bloke didn't take any notice so I just picked it up and carried on playing . . . the run back of the video was like Monty Python, just a complete shambles. They just said, "It's a great act you've got there, boys, throwing the guitars around, that's the spirit!"'

Clearly impressed, Hansa were immediately forthcoming with

the offer of a recording contract, offers also being extended to several others who had responded to the initial advert, among whose number were Japan. Whether the presence of David Sylvian, once described as 'the most beautiful man in pop', in the ranks of the successful set alarm bells ringing is uncertain, but the Easy Cure quickly became suspicious that their looks were more important than their music as far as Hansa were concerned. They were a young, fresh-faced group of five lads, after all, the very material from which teenbeat sensations can be manufactured. Indeed, their anonymous appearance and uniform of jeans and T-shirts provided Hansa with a blank canvas on which they might paint.

The inking of the contract took place five days later in an office suite near Marble Arch, salubrious surroundings designed to impress the youthful groups who were blissfully unaware that the room was being rented by the hour. Nevertheless, Michael Dempsey considered the Hansa contingent to be 'very shifty company' though this didn't prevent the band signing on the dotted line, hardly surprising since capturing a recording contract after just a handful of concerts was the stuff of dreams. Sign in haste, repent at leisure might be a proverb for young bands to remember, however; when the time came to look at the small print, the Easy Cure had committed themselves to Hansa for a £2.50 publishing advance with no retainer. However, their grasp of the need for favourable propaganda would have put Goebbels to shame since, for the consumption of the local press, this was portrayed as a £1000 five-year deal with an imminent single release on Atlantic Records.

Having won a recording contract so easily, increasing misgivings began to be felt by the band as they waited in vain for a call to record this first single. In fact, it was to be almost six months before the Easy Cure were summoned again by which time they had assumed a residency at the Rocket in Crawley, played at an open air show in the town centre – evidence of which opens the *Staring At The Sea* video compilation released in 1986 – and were a far sharper, tougher musical act with a greater sense of direction and purpose. But all was not completely well in the camp. Porl was building upon his reputation as the local guitar hero which meant that all their songs needed to provide him with the opportunity to solo, 'ferociously unpopular at that time', as Michael recounted later. As the band were edging ever further towards punk and new wave with an emphasis on economy and concise expression, Porl was gradually going further and further out on a limb within the group's primitive power structure. More significantly, the Easy Cure found the time to lose yet another singer in September, when O'Toole left to work in Israel just a month before they were due to assemble for their first demo session under Hansa's auspices.

Having landed a recording deal with a five-piece line up, the loss of the focal point of any group, the lead singer, might well have caused other bands to fall apart. The Easy Cure were becoming used to the problem of errant singers, however, and took the loss in their stride. Indeed, O'Toole's departure paved the way for them to accept what had been a gradually dawning realization within the band. Music had initially been a source of entertainment, drinking opportunities and perhaps a little pocket money, but now for Smith, Dempsey, Tolhurst and, to a lesser extent, Thompson, it was becoming a central force in their lives. With Hansa's interest, they were beginning to see that they might have a future in the business, doing something which was very dear to them. O'Toole had just been the latest in a long list of singers who had little to contribute to the group. 'It wasn't his vocation,' noted Dempsey. 'As we started to write more songs, the role of the singer became to convey what the core of us wanted to say. It was because we had singers who were inappropriate that we realized one of us would have to sing.'

Thus did Robert Smith emerge from the ranks to take the leading role in the Easy Cure. It came at the right time, for Smith, though still naive, was sharper than the other members of the band and had been immediately concerned with Hansa's contract and the delay between signing and recording. He had begun to take on a management role of sorts within the band, booking their concerts, for instance, while, in terms of their music, he was becoming an increasingly dominant force, writing the lion's share of their new material. As the main lyricist it was both inevitable and appropriate that Robert should take centre stage yet it was not something which he was desperate to do. He remained a very quiet figure on stage, seemingly shy and a little uncertain of his position in the limelight yet at the same time it was clear that he had great faith both in his own ability and in what he and the group were trying to do. Smith has regularly throughout his career bemoaned the fact that he is not a natural performer though it's something he has come to disguise through the development of a secondary character for concert performance but in these early days, with punk as a backdrop, his diffidence seemed likely to be a terminal drawback.

Hansa certainly seemed to feel the loss of the front-man keenly for when the slimmed-down Easy Cure arrived at London's SAV studios on 11 October the five songs they played met with a frosty reception. 'Meathook', 'See The Children', 'I Just Need Myself', 'I Want To Be Old' and 'Pillbox Tales' – a song which finally surfaced on the B-side to the 1986 version of 'Boys Don't Cry' – did not meet the Hansa brief, the company suggesting that for a session to be held the following month, the band should try a few cover versions. With Smith stuck behind his guitar Hansa clearly felt that their options were being severely reduced and were beginning to get cold feet. The new-look Easy Cure had been busily honing their sound in rehearsal and particularly in live performance and were now a considerably more aggressive prospect than originally, while Robert's shyness tended to translate as surly petulance, not a pose guaranteed to get the teenage girls screaming. Even on the relatively passing acquaint-anceship that Hansa had with the Easy Cure, they knew very clearly that any attempt to force the band to play other material, particularly straightforward chart fodder, would lead to their disenchantment and there seems little doubt that Hansa began a deliberate process of distancing themselves from the Easy Cure with a view to severing relations later in the event of the group failing to meet their unrealistic expectations.

That next session took place on 15 November, again at SAV, and the band played a set of five songs which comprised 'I'm Cold' – a later version of which was used as a B-side to 'Jumping Someone Else's Train' in October 1979 with Siouxsie Sioux contributing backing vocals – a slow take on what was to become their debut release, 'Killing An Arab' as well as 'Little Girl', 'I Saw Her Standing There' and 'Rebel Rebel'. As is so often the case with compromises, nobody was happy with the results, Hansa looking for a more committed pop sound while the group were looking to pursue their own ideas. They became increasingly unhappy with the lack of support which they felt they were receiving from Hansa whose apathetic attitude towards them was rapidly becoming painfully obvious. Hansa clearly felt that something could still be salvaged if only they could talk the Easy Cure into conforming to their Europop ideal while the band's view was the exact opposite. That being so,

Hansa had little inclination to put in any great effort on the group's behalf, though they were still sufficiently hopeful to arrange a further recording session in January 1978 at London's PSL.

The Easy Cure's schedule included a pre-Christmas show at Crawley's Rocket on 4 December which was to ultimately provide the release of the earliest official live Cure material. 'Heroin Face' was recorded at that concert by the four-piece and finally found its way on to *Curiosity* which accompanied the cassette release of *Concert* in 1984. The roughness of that recording illustrates the way the band were developing in different directions with Tolhurst and Dempsey providing a solid, unfussy rhythm, Dempsey emerging as a potentially melodic bassist, with Thompson taking the opportunity to perform a fairly standard hard rock guitar solo, Smith singing in the uninterested monotone typical of the times which he has regularly employed ever since. This one song shows a group that is pulling in several different directions, lacking the necessary cohesive voice and structure that any band with an eye to a recording future requires. The cracks that were beginning to appear in the group between Thompson and the others were clearly widening, no surprise since Smith recalls that Thompson was less than committed during rehearsals, preferring to spend time with Robert's sister whom he was later to marry.

If the group was trying to weather further internal difficulties, its relationship with Hansa was reaching crisis point – a brief listen to that take of 'Heroin Face', indeed simply hearing its title, makes it perfectly clear that Hansa had taken on more than they had bargained for and were unlikely to convert the Easy Cure to their way of thinking particularly as the group were becoming increasingly confident about their musical vision now that Robert had taken over the helm. Having a vocalist who was a real member of the band as opposed to someone passing through had made a great difference to their identity and longer-term plans. It's hard to believe that Robert and the rest of the band were unaware that their attitude would cause problems and that their deal with Hansa was destined to be a short-lived one. By the time of the January session at PSL, the inescapable conclusion is that the Easy Cure were cashing in on the offer of free studio time without any intention of following Hansa's future suggestions.

At PSL, they recorded four songs, reprising 'I Just Need Myself' and Bowie's 'Rebel Rebel' from earlier sessions, going on to tape 'Smashed Up' and 'Plastic Passion', a song which eventually became the B-side to the original version of 'Boys Don't Cry' and again a cursory listen to that song makes it abundantly clear that divorce was on the cards for the Easy Cure and Hansa. To precipitate the irretrievable breakdown, sensing that the time was right to force Hansa's hand, the group suggested that in March, Hansa should release 'Killing An Arab' as their debut single. There were multifarious reasons why Hansa would do no such thing, top among them being that they didn't like the song while they were also gearing up to release the first Japan single, 'Don't Rain On My Parade', around that time. Japan were felt to be a far stronger bet within the record company and there was no way in which they were going to jeopardize their future by becoming distracted with a group who, they were rapidly concluding, were no-hopers. The band were equally exasperated with the lack of progress, viewing Hansa with the same jaundiced eye the record company had cast on them. Robert later commented disgustedly that the idea of 'Killing An Arab' was never seriously considered since 'they said even if it was a good song, they couldn't put it out because we had to keep in with the Arabs!'

Given that they were a band with a rare business intelligence behind them, an intelligence which came largely from Smith, the Easy Cure seized the initiative and forced a break with Hansa who were so glad to be rid of them that they didn't take up the rights to any of the songs or recordings which the group had made to this point, thereby missing out on substantial future royalties, most notably on 'Killing An Arab'. The decree absolute came through on 29 March leaving the Easy Cure free to pursue their interests elsewhere, a state of affairs which left them delighted, clear evidence of the confidence they had in themselves and in their ability to obtain another deal. Few groups of comparable age and experience would be so pleased to have lost a recording contract.

Perhaps the most interesting facet of the Hansa experience is that it provides another insight into the psychology of the Easy Cure and most notably that of Robert Smith, shedding light on his character in much the same way that his views on Notre Dame do – his comments on both organizations reveal more about him than they do about the bodies concerned. Smith's attitude to Hansa has been a broadly antagonistic one over the years and when presented with an opportunity to talk about the company he has rarely let the chance go by without talking of its staff in derogatory terms. Yet, for all their inability to understand just exactly what the Easy Cure were striving for and the low advance which they gave the group, Hansa did provide them with a very useful service, one prized above all else by any up and coming band – free studio time, time to experiment and get to grips with the intricacies of working efficiently and effectively within the highly artificial studio environment. It has been noted already that by the end of the relationship, the Easy Cure were simply taking what they could get from Hansa in terms of recording experience, accumulating valuable knowledge that would be priceless when the time finally came for them to enter a studio with a record company sympathetic to their sound, one keen to promote them correctly.

In dismissing the Hansa attitude, Smith employed his typical blanket condemnation of anyone and everyone associated with the object of his distaste. Hansa's treatment of the group clearly rankled, so much so that even eighteen months later when the group provided a session for David Jensen's Radio 1 show, they put together a parody of a Eurodisco stomp entitled 'Do The Hansa', a vaguely amusing diatribe ostensibly aimed at the evils of commercialism which again surfaced on the 1986 'Boys Don't Cry' single, while 'Meathook' from the debut album also concerned itself with Hansa's attitude.

Although the hard sell production line values of their erstwhile record company may have won them little respect from an act so focused on doing things their own way in their own time, it's churlish none the less simply to refuse to accept that Hansa did assist the development of the Easy Cure. Their perseverance in the face of an almost entirely negative attitude from the band does them some credit but the idea that outsiders might have actually benefited him and helped him to progress is a concept that often seems alien to Smith and is symptomatic of his paradoxical nature – at times he goes to the greatest lengths to make the group seem democratic and a collective where everyone's input is equally vital yet at others he steadfastly refuses to accept that others might have made a contribution. His actions over the years prove that Smith is extremely loyal, even devoted, to those who he feels deserve his friendship and who share his ideals but once the line is crossed he has no compunction in banishing the very thought of them from his mind, a scenario that was to be repeated throughout the next decade, most surprisingly when the time came for Lol Tolhurst to leave the fold. His actions appear to be callous but they are the ethics of a military commander, who has a burning desire to succeed whatever the cost and refuses to be dragged down by others who are, in his opinion, failing to make the appropriate contribution.

Some may point to this as evidence of a protective cloak drawn around a superstar's fragile ego but on reflection it suggests a marked degree of tunnel vision, a singlemindedness or absolute certainty of purpose that would allow no doubts to assail a mind concentrating completely on the job in hand. Smith knew exactly what he wanted to achieve and any acceptance of the influence of an outside agency might cause him to wonder if that was deflecting the band from their original path. It also reflects a characteristic that was part of his upbringing: 'I was brought up to think that if you don't look after yourself no one else will, so right from the start we didn't sign contracts, we've never had a manager because I just thought I could do it without anyone else. The group joins in, everything's divided equally but in the end I have the final say.' Robert has often referred to the early years of the band as 'a crusade', adding that, 'The first five years wasn't like being in a group, it was like waging a war!' The group was formed as a reaction to the musical dross that surrounded them, but Robert's faith in the music and in himself has been such that for the group to succeed as he intends, he cannot allow himself to accept sub-standard work nor people around him who do not have a similar vision. Failure to present the group in a serious manner at its inception would have meant its inevitable demise. Any creeping doubt would have left the group to rot from within with the inevitable consequences.

The one dominant characteristic that has endured down the years is Smith's incredible self-absorption and his inability – or is it simply a refusal? – to relate to things that exist beyond his own sense of self and what he knows of existence. While there is a certain element of tongue in cheek in his attitude, it contains a great deal of truth about the Robert Smith that is compelled to write songs: 'Someone once told me that if I could accept the notion of the world before I was born, I could accept the notion of death . . . I think it's intellectually impossible to conceive the notion of the world before you were born . . . it's a kind of disbelief. I can't genuinely feel that my mom and dad existed before I was born even though I know and everything tells me that they did, I can't be convinced of it deep down . . . Simon [Gallup] got me a video of what happened in 1959. The things that happened before April 1959 I find slightly more unreal than the things that happened after . . . even now, with my own mom and dad, you base it on an element of trust and you think, "What would they gain by fabricating this enormous lie?"' Anyone who is so wrapped up with their own existence is clearly motivated solely by their own impulses and instincts with little consideration for those of outsiders. Reference to his songwriting also suggests that his world is the only world and to an extent such singlemindedness is admirable. After all, as Smith avers, 'The opposite of self-indulgence, trying to be relevant to a vast amount of people, is even more worthless.' In attempting to be honest with himself, being driven by his own criteria with a total disregard for the advice of others, Smith and his group have managed to strike a chord with a mass of people who would love to live life by his credo but who lack the gift, the opportunity or the simple bloody-mindedness to do so. Aiming purely at commercial success, directing his work at the lowest common denominator simply to steal Elton John's audience, would be an unacceptable compromise for Smith and his audience, dishonesty for the sake of financial gain. The bank account might grow but Smith would feel worthless since his view of 'art' is one of absolute honesty to his own ideals.

This clarity of purpose, the knowledge that as well as being a musical force, the Cure is Smith's vehicle for achieving the kind of life he wants to live, has led him to surround himself with like minds, eventually turning the band into a kind of social club. Yet it is a social club with a strictly defined hierarchy; Robert has said, 'I've never been involved with the whole one-of-the-lads scene and things like that.' While the years have seen him carefully insulate himself within a group framework, he admits that 'I haven't got that group sensibility I suppose of belonging or things like that'. From his own isolation, his alienation from the rest of the world, it is Smith's great achievement that he has been able to fashion a lifestyle for himself wherein he can function successfully and can cope with the demands of everyday life. It's become a cliché now, though it's no less true for all that, that such is his horror of the workaday world that stretches beyond Cure-land, had it not been for the Cure, there would have been no other outlet for Smith and his often fragile grasp on his own sanity might not have held. In that way, the Cure has certainly acted as the main channel for unleashing his own emotions and demons, a kind of personal Samaritans, Smith telling *Sounds'* David Hepworth early on that, 'I don't really open up because I used to a lot and . . . there's so few people I've met that I can get on with and that you can trust that I don't see that it's worth it.' When moved, 'I don't throw tantrums or anything like that . . . I go off somewhere rather than smash the room. I write things down. It's a release.' While this intensity has ebbed and flowed over the band's career, and while Smith himself has changed as a person, that passion remains the root of their most powerful music.

Smith clearly has a very low tolerance threshold and refuses to suffer fools gladly, if at all. Like many others of 'artistic temperament', Robert is obsessively concerned with the minutiae of writing and recording music, having an overall concept in mind all the time. He has a razor-sharp musical intelligence and quick wits, and as far as he is concerned those who could not fully understand nor share his artistic vision were worthy of neither his time nor interest. The high turnover of personnel reflects this volatility and the intensity of the demands he places upon his colleagues. Having rarely had any doubts about his own ability and having had a clear-cut idea of exactly what has to be done to achieve the goals he sets for himself, anyone slipping outside these bounds is given short shrift – with the Cure, the ends have always been paramount, the means secondary.

Nineteen-seventy-eight was a crucial year in the development of the Easy Cure. At the end of their tenure with Hansa Robert was quick to realize that they had reached a crossroads in their evolution, a point at which they had either to commit themselves to the group in a more business-like fashion or simply follow it up as a hobby. For Robert there were few doubts by now for the idea of working in any kind of 'normal' job was simply out of the question. His transition to singing had been relatively easy, his limitations easily disguised by the fashion of the day, the idea of non-performance and a depersonalized singing style finding a broad acceptance. As Robert was by now the clear, if unacknowledged, leader of the band the style that they were to follow was very much up to him.

Growing increasingly dissatisfied with Porl's style of guitar playing, which made them resemble a hard rock outfit, as well as his escalating impatience with Porl's attitude to rehearsal, Robert staged the first of what were to be many surreptitious oustings of band members. Meeting secretly with Lol and Michael in the greenhouse of his parents' home, the three concluded that Porl was no longer wanted in the band, his playing too wildly at variance with what the other three were aiming towards. Using the Hansa débâcle as a convenient cover, Robert dissolved the Easy Cure only to reconvene it as a three-piece a couple of weeks later without informing Porl.

Fortunately for all concerned, this was not too egregious a personal blow for Thompson since he too was becoming dissatisfied with his role in the group and was ready to enrol at the West Sussex College of Design for a course which lasted from 1979 to 1981. There were no hard feelings: in July they held a concert called 'Mourning The Departed' which featured a mock seance and which ended with Porl, having watched from the audience in disguise, climbing on stage and pouring beer over Lol, early evidence of Lol's scapegoat role within the band. Interestingly, the concert was set up as Robert's reaction to local fans who were unhappy with Porl's ejection and who wanted the group to retain their rock credentials.

Essentially, Robert felt that the Easy Cure were too rooted in old musical forms while Porl was with them, leading to a musical over-embellishment. He had now decided that they should be paring down the sound, aiming for a more minimalist feel. This move does also lead to the inescapable conclusion that Robert was setting in place the final components of an insurmountable power base within the group, a position from which he could dictate its every move, at least in the short term.

Every band has its own shifting internal dynamic whether they are full blown democracies or based around the ideas and instincts of one out and out leader. Within the confines of rock music the three premier positions are songwriter, lead singer and lead guitarist, the guitarist often being able to build up a personal following beyond the stature of the group itself. With Porl out of the way, Robert was now in sole control of the latter two aspects and was far and away the biggest contributor to the songwriting process; in effect Robert was invulnerable within the group set-up having eliminated the 'guitar hero' and removed any musical obstacles to his plan of slimming down the group's sound. The Easy Cure would also be free of ego problems since Robert's was by now the one that counted for the most.

This is not to say that he was unfair in his treatment of Lol and Michael since songwriting credits and royalties were equally shared on the first album and he paid due homage to their contributions when he began to give newspaper interviews, Nick Kent remarking in *NME* in May 1979 that 'a discussion on who writes what in the Cure democracy features an almost humble Smith – their main muse – delegating responsibilities for the final shaping to the other two as though they were composing equals', intriguing further evidence of

Smith's fractured ego. He is cocooned within his own fierce self-belief and personal security to such an extent that he does not need to, indeed feels it unfair that he should receive, all the credit for the group's work yet, in these early days at least, he clearly believed that only he was capable of steering the good ship Easy Cure, an appropriate analogy for one who is now known throughout the music press as Cap'n Bob. By May 1978, Robert Smith was undoubtedly first among equals and the captain of the ship, so much so that he changed its name from what he felt to be the vaguely hippyish Easy Cure to simply the Cure, a name which was far more fitting for those musical times.

Chapter Three

NEWLY christened, the Cure had now to set their minds to the task of attracting fresh record company activity, interest this time from a like-minded company who would allow the group the artistic freedom upon which they would insist. The inescapable conclusion drawn by the slimmed down trio was that they should go back to the drawing board and come up with a new demo tape to send out to all the major players in London. Similarly inescapable was the conclusion that they couldn't afford to make such a tape – a few local concerts were barely enough to build up band funds and so they set about looking for sponsors within their coterie.

In their locale the Cure had to share their celebrity with a band called Lockjaw who had already released a couple of singles, 'Radio Call Sign' and 'Journalist Jive', both of which sank without trace, deservedly so according to their bass player Simon Gallup. Lockjaw were a more straightforward punk group than the Cure but the two bands regularly played together and it was in the course of those engagements that Smith and Gallup spent long periods of time in one another's company, drinking copiously, a hobby that has persisted to this very day. Simon was ultimately to play a central role in the future of the Cure but it was his brother Ric who was to have an impact first of all.

Introduced to the Cure when seeing them play with his brother's group, Ric became a fan and felt that they had the potential to go on and make records for national rather than local consumption. Seeing that they were in an impossible situation financially and realizing that since they were restricted to playing local gigs only they were unlikely to gain attention that way, Ric financed a demo session that cost around £50, a debt of gratitude they were able to repay some years later when they funded his film, *Carnage Visors*. Selecting songs carefully from their burgeoning repertoire, the Cure entered Chestnut Studios in Frensham, Sussex, on 27 May 1978 and demoed 'It's Not You', 'Fire In Cairo', '10.15 Saturday Night', which was proving to be their most popular live song, and 'Boys Don't Cry', an obvious choice as their most engaging and commercially viable piece of idiot pop.

This demo version of 'Boys Don't Cry' ultimately found its way onto *Curiosity* and forms an interesting contrast with that which was finally released as a single a year later. The song itself was a vindication of Robert's vision of a simpler sound, for it was a song that could so easily have been ruined by any ornamentation. Basically 'Boys Don't Cry' was the essence of new wave, the perfect pop single, economical and direct, an updated version of the Beatles' halcyon pop period around *Rubber Soul*. The demo did leave something to be desired, however, the faltering vocal being smothered by studio effects while Robert's guitar figure lacked the cutting edge that later recordings possessed. The band as a whole sounded composed, Lol's playing perhaps a little too busy for a song that required space, but clearly there was potential within this group. The most remarkable thing about the session, however, was the songs. If 'It's Not You' smacked of album filler material the other three illustrated a potent pop sensibility at work, one which was able to select the most enduring elements of punk and graft them onto what they had extracted from previous eras. Unlike Johnny Rotten, the Cure did not sneer at the Beatles but instead, and far more intelligently for any group aiming at longevity, borrowed from them and from other past masters. If the tape had one abiding feature it was the eloquent demonstration of their ability, particularly that of Robert, to absorb and assimilate an astounding range of music, sift through it to discard anything superfluous and distil the remainder into a package that was at once original and yet oddly familiar.

Popular mythology would have us believe that punk did away with the old attitudes as firmly as did the French Revolution, record companies applauding loudly in their ignorance as ELP pronounced that the punks should eat cake moments before they were consigned to that bargain bin in the sky. Popular mythology is of course complete nonsense as the current sorry state of British music indicates – it's as if punk never happened, as one book has already had it. Though it pretends to be creative, the record industry is reactive, desperately following trends and trying to turn them into money before fashion moves on and so all that the new wave did was to cause one of the regular outbreaks of panic within the corporate industry, the valium for which is to clone the shock of the new to death. By the middle of 1978 each and every record label had its own Sex Pistols, most of whom were thoroughly dreadful without the slightest spark of originality, ideal for record moguls who are always uneasy among artists who can think for themselves. This is of course the central reason why trends are so often short-lived since after the initial spark, all the public is fed is safe, second-rate rubbish which soon goes stale.

The inevitable consequence of this industry indolence is that the most vital music often tends to come from the independent sector where the content rather than the packaging is the central theme. Anything different, anything displaying fresh ideas or a new approach is greeted only with suspicion by the majors while the indies welcome it with open arms. Since the Cure's demo tape had much about it that was new, most notably the dispassionate vocal that had still to gain mainstream acceptance, the major record labels all passed on the tape. After all, they had already house-trained a new wave group and didn't need any further groups of that sort while no doubt some had heard of the Easy Cure's dealings with Hansa on the industry grapevine and had them marked down as trouble-makers to whom it was wisest to give a wide berth. As the rejection slips dropped through Smith's letterbox with monotonous regularity there was growing despondency within the camp who were beginning to wonder about their next move.

A&R men fulfil an odd role inside the record company. Their job is to spot original and marketable talent and then wait and hope that their masters act on it, a frustrating role when you are forced to wait for the wheels of a blinkered industry to grind their way to a decision. Some of the species ultimately give up the good fight and pick up administrative roles or simply leave. Others use their ability and knowledge to come up with their own method of working in the industry, backing their judgement and behaving in what those around them perceive to be a maverick fashion. One such was Chris Parry, who worked as Polydor's A&R Department Manager in the mid-seventies having emigrated to the UK from his native New Zealand in 1970. Parry stood out in particular since he had a decidedly contemptuous regard for careerism and the compromises necessary to make the way up the greasy corporate pole. Parry worked for Polydor because he was a music fan not a businessman, though he was not short of financial acumen.

Like so many of his ilk he was startled by the onset of punk but unlike the majority of his contemporaries he found the whole thing exciting and revelled in the music that this plethora of new bands were making. Quick to translate this incredible rush of energy into recording potential, he recommended both the Sex Pistols and the Clash to Polydor only to see the hierarchy there refuse to back his judgement, a galling situation given that for several years new talent had been at a premium. Another of Parry's favourites were Siouxsie and the Banshees who were just starting to make their presence felt around London. He spent a great deal of time persuading Polydor to sign them, a quest that was finally successful. Parry's stocks were by then particularly high within the company since it was he, on the advice of Shane McGowan, later of the Pogues, who had signed the Jam, who had already scored four Top Forty singles and two Top Thirty albums by the time the Cure's tape found its way to his desk. However, it was not a reciprocal arrangement for Parry was very quickly growing very tired of the Polydor hit factory and the production-line values that are essential to oil the wheels of any major corporation. The response time, the channels of command, the organizational structures, the myriad departments in charge of each individual aspect of a group's career all jarred. The need to follow these formalized structures robbed records of their spontaneity and often of their relevance – pop is by definition ephemeral and so the response time of the record business has to be fast. The major label rendered such an idea impossible. Parry was rapidly concluding that the best way to make records was to run his own independent label that could act with the alacrity for which he was searching.

Even so, when he first approached the Cure it was under the Polydor banner, clearly aware of the kudos that that name would carry with a group of young hopefuls. Naturally delighted that anyone should be showing an interest in them, especially an established major label, Robert called Parry's secretary as requested and showing his rapidly maturing self-confidence and business nous, immediately refused Parry's offer to play a London concert – an intelligent if daring refusal since the band had never played within the capital and so would be forced to perform a crucial gig before an uninterested audience. Inviting the band to meet him at Polydor, Parry quickly endeared himself to them by buying drinks at the nearest pub. It soon became evident that there was common ground between himself and the band and Parry left impressed with their attitude and particularly that of Robert who, while covering his initial disappointment at the suggestion that they sign to an independent rather than Polydor itself, took this perceived reverse in his stride and grilled Parry at length on his objectives for such a label and how the Cure might fit into the scheme of things.

By this very early stage in their career, Robert was already earning himself a thoroughly deserved reputation as the business head in the Cure organization having been the prime mover in the successful defection from Hansa with publishing rights intact and now being very clearly in charge of negotiations with any future record company. If the future was to see him portrayed as some helpless waif or stray, his off-stage activities show him to be something very different and it's clear that he is happy to play up to this paradox when the occasion suits. If Smith likes to play the fool, and he is entirely right in describing the Cure as 'a very foolish band', when circumstances dictate he is nobody's fool. Unlike many contemporaries, Robert uses his intelligence and common sense to create an environment for himself in which he can act according to whim; it is a space that has been hard won and one which he refuses to jeopardize.

If disappointed that the Cure weren't set to find a home on Polydor, Robert was quick to weigh up the possibilities that Parry's suggestions offered and was equally quick to look at the advantages, especially in terms of personnel devoted almost exclusively to the Cure, and the chance to shape the company in the way in which he wanted. This mode of attack also provided flexibility and a degree of financial independence while still making use of all the advantages of Polydor's distribution and marketing resources. In short, Smith concluded that to be an independent within the heart of the industry was precisely the position for a free spirit like himself. Once Parry had seen the group in action, the die was cast, the Cure turning down his offer to sign them to Polydor if they preferred, choosing to throw in their lot with his company. After some debate, Fiction was selected as its name, Robert having refused to sign if Parry persisted with his original suggestion, 18 Age.

It was at this point that one of the popular misconceptions that surround the Cure came into play. Contrary to the accepted view, the Cure have never employed Chris Parry in the role of group manager – he is categorically not their manager, for as Robert noted, '[He] likes to think he's our manager but he isn't. Any group with an ounce of common sense doesn't need a manager . . . we don't pay him anything. He takes his money as owner of Fiction when we sell records. I made it very clear to him at the beginning that it was in his interest that we should sell lots of records.' This has ultimately become a highly satisfactory arrangement for both parties, since Parry now holds a controlling interest – he is one of two shareholders along with his PA, Ita Martin – in a very successful recording company, while his contract of employment with Fiction entitles him to 95 per cent of the profits of the company, payable on a quarterly basis. Over the course of the four years from the beginning of 1989 to the end of 1992, for instance, the chairman of Fiction Records received around £1.1 million for his efforts, additional to which were healthy contributions into the company pension scheme for the directors which totalled around £600,000 over the same period – and Parry has just one co-director, Martin again.

Parry's vision in signing the Cure and his ability to work with Robert Smith throughout his assortment of psychological and physiological ups and downs has eventually brought its own financial rewards. Fiction is by no means a Thatcherite model, giving £147,000 to charity in the year to 31 December 1991. It is a thoroughly solid company with assets that would attract a host of potential buyers should Parry ever feel like early retirement, all of which is a far cry from its position in the early eighties when the Cure were struggling to sell records and their erratic behaviour left the company in a straitened financial position.

Robert's statement that he was keen to sell as many records as possible without that dictating the group's sound also blows away the myth that he has wanted the Cure to remain a sheltered little cult band – he has always had his eyes on the global horizon with the ambition to infiltrate the charts world-wide, admitting later, 'When we started I didn't enjoy being in a cult band, but I realized why we were because I despised everything in the charts.' Success, however, has always had to be gained on his own terms without compromise simply because 'you have to have some success mentally as well as physically because you've got to think that people are appreciating what you're doing. You can't change just for that because it wouldn't be much fun if you had success and then people saw through it and started to move away from you.'

From the outset, though, Smith has always had his sights set on becoming successful, if only to sustain himself in a life beyond the norm and with Fiction, he saw the way forward, commenting in 1985 that, 'The transition [towards commercial success] has been slow but comfortable, exactly how I wanted it. Same label, the same people working for us, just gradually getting bigger in manageable steps that are controlled on the way.' It is obvious that Smith has controlled those steps, just as it is obvious that little in the Cure's commercial evolution has been left to chance. Musically, of course, things have been different with outside influences always playing a part.

Having agreed an initial six-month deal with Fiction in September, providing them each with a wage of £25 per week, the Cure began to up their live schedule combining concerts with ad hoc visits to Morgan Studios to record their debut LP. At one such concert, the band were support act to Wire, an experience which changed Smith's perception and expectations of his band, helping him give a form to the next musical steps which he intended to take. Wire were the acme of the acne-ridden new wave, a tight, economical, powerful band that came across as a dramatic live group, turning concerts into more than a series of songs but consuming, enveloping events. Their simple arrangements and reductive approach left Smith depressed by the inevitable comparisons with his group, yet excited by the possibilities such a group opened up. If Parry had signed up a pop group, the Cure were a pop group no longer.

The greatest question of the time was, just why had Parry signed the Cure to head his new label? Certainly there were obvious parallels to be drawn with his great discovery, the Jam. Both had songs that were urgent, poppy and clearly commercial while the bands themselves were young, fresh-faced and eminently presentable. As lead singer, Parry felt that Smith had the necessary charisma to project the group while his clear vision, a quality he had previously identified in Paul Weller, boded well for the longevity of the group. Fiction Records were not simply interested in taking on the Cure at face value, however, for Robert recalls, 'In the first year . . . Fiction and Chris Parry were trying to mould us into this new young three-piece. It took us a year to make him realize that we were scruffy and wilful.' Hansa had left its mark on the Smith psyche and the hint of compromise was something he would refuse to countenance. 'I'm very hard-headed and I know what I want to do and if I get something in my mind I do it regardless of what anybody says, record company, media, anybody.' Any attempts that Parry might have made to become the Cure's Svengali were doomed to failure from the outset and the Wire experience merely served to confirm Robert's view of the long-term direction of his group.

Despite these sizeable reservations as to their current set, there was an album to be recorded first and the time-scale was such that it provided no opportunity to write new material. The first session, on 20 September 1978, yielded five songs, the title-track 'Three Imaginary Boys' plus 'Killing An Arab', '10.15 Saturday Night', 'Fire In Cairo', and 'Plastic Passion'. The group as a whole were unhappy with these sessions which saw Parry in the producer's chair, largely because they, Robert particularly, felt that their sovereign right to be sole arbiters of the band's sound was being taken from them by outside forces who wanted them to become something they weren't.

On the other side, Parry was quickly exasperated by a group who felt they knew best when clearly they were at sea in the studio, and who were refusing to upgrade their equipment to that suitable for a recording environment. Smith maintained that their cheap sound was what he was looking for, citing Costello's *My Aim Is True* as precedent. Both felt they were acting for the best reasons, Robert steadfast in the knowledge that only he knew what he wanted to do and what would suit his group while Parry was equally determined to steer them away from the punk waters, his international experience telling him that it would mean little beyond the confines of the UK and that any group with its eyes on wider exposure would have to employ greater subtlety. His early sightings of the Cure had excited him because 'they were very musical, almost rootless, which made them very contemporary'. It was this musicality that he wished to encourage, a move which Robert frowned upon.

There were further teething troubles in these early months as the band attempted to come to terms with life as a professional group, getting themselves ejected from an allegedly prestigious support tour with Generation X in December. Personality differences began to surface both internally and between the group and Parry, who was keen to fabricate some kind of accessible, acceptable image for the group while they had no interest in becoming fashion victims. Given Smith's self-confessed stubbornness and Parry's determination to get his label off to a flying start with his own methods, it could have been a case of the immovable object and the irresistible force had it not been for Parry's one ace – he was paying for everything and the band were indebted to him. For that reason alone, Parry had the final say though he made attempts at compromise by introducing Mike Hedges to the sessions, a young engineer of similar age, experience and outlook to the Cure who was required to act as go-between.

Ultimately the band had to go along with most of Parry's suggestions, a situation which left an indelible mark and ensured that the future operations of the Cure would be very different. Again Smith was fast to realize that for as long as he owed money he would be forced to dilute his artistic vision for commercial considerations. He and the rest of the band resolved that their future earnings from the group would first of all be channelled into recording their next album. 'He who pays the piper calls the tune' was a lesson learned, Smith noting that, 'We never borrow from the record company which frustrates them because it means they can't tell us what to do.' He later complained that Polydor's lack of promotion of the album he and Steve Severin recorded as *The Glove* in 1983 was an act of revenge on their part against Smith's prudent financial dealings.

The album was finished off with a marathon two-day stint in mid-October that left everyone shattered and Robert dissatisfied with the finished product. The saving grace of the whole project was that at least it confirmed that the Cure were up and running and, with the record out of the way, they could fully occupy themselves with writing new songs between touring commitments. After all, all their debut required was promoting and packaging.

Chapter Four

ROBERT had already made clear his love of John Peel's nightly show on Radio 1, often noting that his greatest ambition was to get Peel to play one of his records. The trio's exploits in and around London won them something even better, the offer of a much sought-after session spot to be recorded in December 1978, before they had even released a single, never mind an album, an encouraging sign that the Cure were beginning to make their presence felt within the most influential of circles. More importantly, certainly for internal confidence, the Peel session proved that the band were right about their musical philosophy. The Peel session which comprised the inevitable quartet of 'Killing An Arab', '10.15 Saturday Night', 'Fire In Cairo' and 'Boys Don't Cry', their strongest material to date, was a triumph and stands as the definitive version of those songs, realizations far superior to their released counterparts. The sound was rougher, more aggressive and was fondly remembered by all those who took part, Dempsey agreeing that they 'captured the spirit . . . I found that the producers [Tony Wilson with engineer Dave Dade] had exactly the right approach: if it looked like you knew what you were doing, they just let you get on with it.'

The session certainly lit some kind of spark around the Cure within the industry, a useful adjunct to the early notices they were getting for their live shows, the first *NME* piece being filed the same month. Everything was ready for the band to release their first single, but Fiction was unable to do so since Polydor had yet to agree the distribution deal with Parry. To ensure that the single reached the shops amid this publicity, Small Wonder, a small East London label, were given the opportunity to release 'Killing An Arab'/'10.15 Saturday Night'. A licence for 15,000 copies was agreed, a number which, if sold, would finance a similar number on Fiction after

Christmas. If a less than perfect set-up, it did at least provide a useful method of market testing without too great a financial risk being incurred. Stocks sold out quickly, enabling Fiction to reissue the single as their first release in February 1979.

Perhaps Fiction chose to release a record with such a potentially provocative title in order to gain notoriety and publicity or perhaps it was simply issued as the band's most insistent and idiosyncratic pop song – musically it certainly stood out from the crowd, having the prerequisite degree of aggression essential for the time but a quirky, almost sixties pop sensibility that linked it to the Kinks' school of English whimsicality. With its eastern intro, a geographical reply perhaps to the Banshees' 'Hong Kong Garden', it caught the attention immediately but it was its lyric that garnered most attention. Smith affected incomprehension that the song could be misinterpreted, though the truth of the matter was forcibly brought home to him when a gig at the Nashville in London was disrupted by a National Front member who perceived the group to be fellow-racists. The record was rarely played beyond the confines of late-night radio and therefore missed any chance of a chart placing, the first controversy stirred up by a song that was to come up against censorship difficulties time and again through the years, most laughably when Radio 1 deemed it unsuitable during the Gulf War. In America problems arose with the issue of the *Standing On A Beach* compilation, itself a line from the song, when the American company wanted to delete the song from the running order, a suggestion that appalled Smith who refused point blank to consider the idea, even going so far as to contact Arab groups in the US to explain what the song was actually about.

'Killing An Arab' was a throwback to Smith's schooling and the early days of the Cure, being a piece based on Albert Camus's *The Outsider* which he had encountered while taking French 'A' level – again this brings up his spurious denials of any past influences. If anything has characterized Smith's lyrics right through the history of the Cure, it is that they are not hidebound by convention but are often experimental or exploratory, something which calls to mind his schooling at Notre Dame while his studies in the sixth form at St Wilfrid's obviously left their mark, giving him an abiding interest in French literature, with Baudelaire also serving as source material for later work.

If the racist storm was whipped up intermittently through their career, the real legacy of 'Killing An Arab' was to cast the Cure as the new existentialists, abstract modernist commentators on life's absurdities. It was a stance which attracted a bout of newspaper feeding frenzy, and which the group maintained over the forthcoming years, yet an image which had little relevance to them as people. After the release of the single, it was clear that the group hadn't appreciated that they would have to offer explanations to prevent the song's misinterpretation, and they quickly found themselves in a situation where they were dropping Camus's name as if they were old pals, Smith suggesting that he was attracted to the story because it 'has really good imagery with bright light and pain'. To discuss such a writer in the context of a press interview was strange enough but the Cure were forced into a situation whereby they had to continually reiterate the basis for the song to take the sting from the racist jibes. It might have been better had they quoted from *The Outsider*, 'the whole world seemed to have come to a standstill on this little strip of sand between the sunlight and the sea . . . And just then it crossed my mind that one might fire, or not fire – and it would come to absolutely the same thing'. Immediately the Cure, particularly their enigmatic singer, were intellectuals, great philosophers with piercing insights into the human condition. Smith was thrown off balance by this unexpected development, complaining to *Sounds* that, 'It's ridiculous, you put out a record that's greeted with some measure of acclaim and you're immediately in a position where people should listen to you . . . I don't really see myself as one of the top three original thinkers in the world today so I'm not in any position to expound my philosophy of life.'

'Killing An Arab' was basically an extension of the themes of what was to be the first Cure album: boredom, ennui and a sense of futility, broadly the themes that had been examined by a host of other new wave riders, albeit in a generally less intelligent or stimulating manner. Ironically, at the time, Chris Parry was worried that the group were enjoying themselves too much and wanted to inject a little gravitas into the proceedings – 'Killing An Arab' achieved that to an extent beyond his wildest dreams and eventually did the group little good, for it was to be many years before they were able to shed some of the heavyweight intellectual and emotional baggage that it foisted upon them. Matters were not helped by the desolate '10.15 Saturday Night' on the B-side which *NME*'s Nick Kent described as 'something of an isolated vignette, hopefully portraying a whole mood of rejection', such a preposterous piece of criticism that Robert took to repeating it to journalists who asked him about the song. Nevertheless '10.15', while in a sense commercial with its engaging hook, was faintly depressing in tone and scarcely promoted the idea of the band as jovial popsters.

At the time the single first saw the light of day, on record at least the Cure were a fairly lightweight power-pop group, if already a very good one. 'Boys Don't Cry', released in June, endeavoured to redress the balance with its glorious idiot pop attack, a song which lead to comparisons with Manchester's Buzzcocks, Smith and Pete Shelley having undeniably similar voices. But by this time, few were listening with open minds since the Cure had released their debut LP which had left them firmly ensconced in what was termed the mope-rock scene, alongside Joy Division.

That such an attitude came to prevail underlines the incredible importance of marketing, promotion and packaging. Exasperated by a group that had little interest in promoting themselves and even less in promoting any kind of image, Parry chose to use that as the group's selling point. Using his financial hold over the group as his main weapon, Parry presented them with the album artwork for *Three Imaginary Boys*, produced by Bill Smith. There were no pictures of the group but instead the three members were represented by mundane household objects – a fridge, a vacuum cleaner and a lampstand. Taking the levels of absurdity still further, there were no song titles listed but visual clues were given instead such as a burnt postcard of the pyramids for 'Fire In Cairo' or the bags of sugar that inspired the lyric for 'So What'.

The reactions of Dempsey, Tolhurst and Smith to the cover illustrated each's role within the band's structure but also highlighted the damaging cracks that were starting to appear within the relationships. Michael Dempsey felt that the cover concept was quite successful, suggesting that it allowed the Cure to grasp a mystique without embracing any lurking pretension, while Lol characteristically tried to make the best of things by reinforcing Parry's official line. Robert was horrified by the whole thing, not least because he had had no input into the sleeve at all. Recognizing that people do judge a book, and a record for that matter, by its cover, he felt that the sleeve would do nothing but damage and was embarrassed by every aspect of it, the same aspects that Parry felt were so strong. With such irreconcilable differences at work, Parry simply pressed on regardless and quickly received the response he had been looking for. Intrigued by this novel kind of presentation coming in the wake of the 'Killing An Arab' furore, reviews were generally based on an idea of the band rather than the music they had produced. The Cure were held up as re-inventors of rock music, innovative geniuses with the answers to life, the universe and everything, while the media in the form of *Sounds*' Dave McCullough turned Parry into 'that essential fourth Cure. Producer, mentor, minder, keeper . . . the undoubted epicentre of the Cure . . . the figure that walks and provides the ostensibly decadent, *Dark Side Of The Moon*ish packaging gimmicks that furnish and inevitably and intriguingly both denigrate the album and perversely enhance its cheaper charms . . . a witty metaphor.'

Smith's reaction to Parry's work on the debut album, both as producer and marketer, indicates just how wrapped up in his own world he was. With no management deal with the band to fall back on, Parry had to commit himself to the successful development of his new record label, a label whose roster was headed by the Cure. At that point in time, it was essential for Parry to ensure that sales of and interest in his new artists were maximized if there was to be any chance of long-term growth in his label. If Smith was solely and selfishly preoccupied with artistic concerns, Parry had to ensure that money was going to flow into the company bank account. Failure to do so would mean no company and potential financial ruin for Parry while Smith and the Cure might simply have been able to move to another label, perhaps to Polydor itself.

Parry's attempts to stimulate interest, perhaps clumsy for some tastes, were successful and gave the band a Top Fifty debut LP, a reasonable achievement for a record that was treated as if it were complex and difficult to listen to. However, for one so focused on creating his own reality from his own talents, it's unlikely that Smith was magnanimous about such praise as McCullough's being lavished on Parry. In these early days when his intense concentration on turning the Cure into a long-term project blocked out all else, Smith rarely took kindly to others sharing the limelight, or more particularly to distorting his vision of the group and what they were about. Parry never again enjoyed that kind of freedom, either musically – he was banned from subsequent sessions – or in marketing terms. In public Smith refused to castigate others, though the backhanded compliment was never far from the surface, suggesting that, 'It was good in a way that Chris did produce [*Three Imaginary Boys*] because it threw a perspective on the songs that we'd never seen before and so we could always see how we wanted to develop.' However, behind closed doors, Smith wanted to make his authority crystal clear, a point perceptively made in a *Melody Maker* live review by Van Goss: 'Despite his reputation as Mr Self-effacing & Reticent, Robert Smith looks from here to be quite the hard man who knows what he wants and usually gets it.' Compromise was one of the few words not in the extensive Smith vocabulary and anything that was tainted with the idea had to be dismissed as inadequate.

Actually, *Three Imaginary Boys* was an interesting if uneven debut and certainly a long way from being the classic that it was hailed as. It was a naive, fairly innocent collection of songs which encompassed a variety of moods, some more convincingly than others. An honest, unpretentious record, it was exactly what it sounded, just some songs written by young men in their late teens who had experienced little beyond the confines of suburban life and who were uninspired by the prospect of an ordinary life of clocking in and out of work. This was not studied boredom but rather an honest response to their lives to that point, lives which would normally have been guided into suitable little pigeonholes by the system. The only difference between the Cure and countless others of their generation was that they were turning that bordeom on its head to fuel an alternative way of life and to communicate, as much with themselves as any abstract concept of a wider audience.

Early reviewers of the group had realized that the Cure had more about them than much of the new wave but were more circumspect in their praise, Jon Savage noting that, 'The past is plundered, rewritten and reassembled to be bought and danced to . . . the Cure do so with commendable understatement and integrity.' However, by this time the publicity machine had done its best (or worst, depending on your viewpoint); the album was heralded as 'a masterful debut' in Ian Birch's *Melody Maker* review entitled 'The Eighties Start Here', wherein he termed the LP 'so practical, purposeful and democratic . . . [displaying] comprehensive originality of approach'. Yet all the obvious reference points were on display – Hendrix (including a decidedly ropey cover version of 'Foxy Lady'), the Beatles, Stones, Kinks, Pistols, Buzzcocks – and so to call it comprehensively original was stretching a point beyond breaking. What the Cure's debut did have was glittering promise thanks to its intelligent distillation of these influences allied to its startling economy – where other groups might have fleshed out the sound with rhythm guitar or synths, the Cure left space for the imagination with articulate arrangements.

Smith professed to hate the record instantly and in the light of what followed, it's easy to understand his reservations as he described it as 'a compilation, it didn't have a lot to do with what we were doing even at that time', a reference to his plans for the next Cure record. But that is to ignore the good things that came out of it – 'Fire In Cairo' and 'Three Imaginary Boys' still regularly turn up in their live set even now, and indeed the title track did suggest the next step for the group with its sparse instrumentation and desolate lyric. 'So What' encapsulated the overall feeling of resigned boredom that songs like 'Another Day' also covered, with Robert reciting an offer for an icing set from the back of a packet of sugar, illustrating the futility and absurdity of making records, a trick that others such as Michael Stipe have since borrowed. With 'Subway Song', the Cure repaid their debt to the Sensational Alex Harvey Band with its overblown sense of the theatrical, ending in a less than terrifying scream but proving that all was not doom and gloom in their camp and that they did have a sharp sense of humour, albeit of a fairly dark flavour.

'Grinding Halt' was an impressive showcase of Michael Dempsey's bass playing, the opening being reminiscent of 'Echo Beach', a hit for Martha and the Muffins. Perhaps the similarity prompted thoughts of a single release for white labels of the song were distributed to press and radio before it was shelved because of the poor feedback it received. 'Grinding Halt' was also used as another of the group's attempts to hit back at criticism they felt was unfounded, Robert changing the lyrics on a BBC session to attack Paul Morley, admittedly a sensible hobby for any aspiring group to take up, though it smacked of pettiness. Mention of Dempsey's fluent style was made in the majority of reviews and he quickly took up a position of virtual equality with Robert in the minds of critics since they felt that his melodic style was the fulcrum of the sound, rooting the music within the pop field while providing Robert with the stage and scope to express himself more fully. The general impression was that, commercially at least, their only encumbrance might be Robert's monotone drawl.

The Cure paradox had taken up residence within the music business by now. On the one hand they were warmly commended for their merging of sixties pop and post-punk sensibility into a commercially viable proposition, and yet in the same breath they were categorized as gloom and doom merchants dealing purely in shades of grey, intellectual giants dabbling in the meaning of life. The cornerstone song for that particular perception of the trio was 'Accuracy', a very nasty song about a sour relationship dealing with the minutiae of manipulation to the benefit of neither party. A song that twisted the knife, it took Robert's preoccupation with minimalism to a new level, with its sparse lyric and even more restrictive melody, a masterpiece of repetition and dark introspection. Of the songs that appeared on *Three Imaginary Boys*, this is perhaps the only one that might have realistically survived the editing process for *Seventeen Seconds*, their second album.

Listened to again with the benefit of hindsight, the most striking feature of the record is just how linear were Robert's lyrical ideas and how clearly defined were the songs. Going through each individual track, they all have concise, simple ideas, broadly expressing general truths about life and relationships, so much so in fact that they were occasionally prosaic and flirted dangerously with cliché. Perhaps it is annoyance with this that has coloured his view of the record rather than the input of others for he has never again fallen into the same trap. Indeed, he has been criticized since for being oblique and incomprehensible, a charge he refutes by confirming that he makes records only for himself and that his lyrics communicate their message to him perfectly well. Already noted, his refusal to open up to other people for fear that they will abuse his trust has changed the style and content of his lyric writing to the point at which they are sometimes solipsistic, and he may well believe in retrospect that explicit expositions of his state of mind were not helpful. Oddly, this lucidity, perfectly suited to the pop market, had little effect on perceptions of the band which had them marked down as miserable, inveterate hurlers of toys from prams.

Part of this could be ascribed to what was perceived as generally sulky behaviour whenever they were on public display, as was the case when they made their first video, for '10.15 Saturday Night', a product of misunderstandings rather than intent, as Smith explained. 'We turned up with these ideas and the director was there and said, "We've got two hours, there are your instruments, get on with it." So we thought it was a rehearsal and we went away and we waited six months to do it for real! We just had this po-faced look whenever we were overwhelmed by how stupid everyone was, how drab it was. That's how we got this reputation for being sullen. It was politeness because we didn't want to openly laugh at people.'

Smith, and to some extent Tolhurst and Dempsey, were beginning to feel as if some of the enjoyment was disappearing from the whole experience and took a break through part of the summer of 1979. During this time, Robert didn't remain idle but instead worked on some new music and decided that he would set up his own local label with the help of Ric Gallup again, calling it Dance Fools Dance. Their first release provided an opportunity for two local eleven-year-olds who formed a pot-banging duo called the Obtainers. Their 'Yeh Yeh Yeh' and 'Pussy Wussy' took up one side of the record while the other was given over to two songs, 'Lifeblood' and 'Bombs' by the Magspies, a band featuring Simon Gallup on bass, an enterprise that was to prove to be something of a turning point for the group's personnel.

Over the same period of time, Robert also recorded another one-off single with local postman Frank Bell called 'I'm A Cult Hero', a single that eventually came out on Fiction in December of 1979. Most significantly, however, he recruited Gallup to play bass on what was a light-hearted recording session for which Porl Thompson was once again roped in and which gave Smith the freedom to let off steam after the building pressures of the preceding months. This particular session, though faintly disguised as just knockabout fun, was the culmination of various plans that Robert had been running through his mind to shake up the Cure once more to illustrate to the outside world that it was in the process of further change.

Robert and Simon had been spending increasing amounts of time in one another's company, going out drinking together on a fairly regular basis when Robert's commitments with the Cure would allow. They formed a strong friendship at exactly the point when relations between Smith and Dempsey were on a downward slope, Michael finding little to admire in Robert's new songs while he in turn came to dislike the bass player's more extravagant work, looking as he constantly was to strip down the sound as opposed to ornamenting it. Returning from holiday, Michael found that Simon had been taught the bassline for 'Cult Hero'. Michael was subsequently relegated to playing some meaningless synth, because Robert hadn't yet worked out how to fire him from the band, particularly as they had some summer shows in the offing.

Chapter Five

THE ANNUAL Reading Festival is often a pretty depressing business for unknown groups who are often relegated to dodging urine-filled missiles rather than concentrating on their music but 1979's appearance saw the Cure gaining good responses from audiences who generally knew little or nothing about them. While he might have gained some consolation from this boost to their popularity, Smith was viewing the future of the band with a fairly jaundiced eye and had similarly mixed feelings about the up-coming guest slot they had won on the Siouxsie and the Banshees tour of Britain.

If we are to accept the principle that Robert Smith effectively was and is the Cure, and it's a principle that in his less self-effacing moments he has broadly confirmed, then that has implications for those that surround him. In one respect, it is by virtue of his gifts that the others have been able to continue a career in music – certainly none of those ejected from the band in its long history have achieved anything approaching a similar level of success away from the Cure. That being the case it is perhaps only fair that Robert should be able to construct a group made up along similar lines to a school gang or a drinking club where only those socially compatible are allowed access. However, that denigrates the input that many individuals have made to the band, as musicians, songwriters and confidants. It is significant that even after all this time, Smith has never yet resorted to that stand-by of the ego-tripping rock-star, the solo album. Smith did record one for his own benefit, but refused to sanction any subsequent public release. Again and again his drive, direction and complete faith in his own vision shine through, almost alarmingly at times. He is now perfectly at ease with the idea of coaxing contributions from less certain members of the troupe, though this generosity of spirit is a function of his veto over the group's activities.

Maturity is not a word often bandied around Smith's strikingly coiffed head and it's a word from whose application he might shrink, but as a musician and songwriter Smith has found the necessary maturity of ego and sensibility to recognize that his best work is done within the group format. *The Top*, 1984's Cure opus, is regarded even now with some revulsion by Smith and the roots of its inconsistency lie in the fact that, drums aside, he did almost everything else on the record with no input or criticism from outside sources. That understanding goes back a long way into Cure history, to their very earliest days as recording artists – Dempsey's bass playing was a very important factor in the critical success of *Three Imaginary Boys*, its melodic quality catching the attention of many reviewers. Similarly through much of the Cure's career, Lol Tolhurst played a vital role as bridge-builder between individuals and then as safety valve for the band's frustrations. It was not until Smith himself had gone through a change in his outlook and personality that he considered jettisoning Tolhurst from the group.

Smith undoubtedly has an arresting personality. Even on stage where he is often awkward, cumbersome and patently uncomfortable it's easy to see just how so much of his audience find themselves attracted to him and his music, such is his strength of character and purpose, even if that stage character is a highly distorted version of the Smith that writes the music away from publicity's glare. It is this steely determination that has eventually steered the Cure through to their present pre-eminence and his success could be deemed to justify his almost exclusively selfish means of attaining it. If he feels that there are undesirable elements within the band, who is to argue with the talented auteur who claims that their presence might bring the whole edifice crashing down and that they therefore have to go?

Smith had clearly decided to oust Dempsey in favour of his friend Simon Gallup. The two got on well, enjoyed one another's company and, as importantly, had a degree of musical empathy that no longer existed between Smith and Dempsey for Smith's desire for change had musical reasons that were as strong as personal ones. Indeed, he was not alone in his discomfort for Dempsey too was beginning to question his place within the scheme of things, admitting later that,

'I wasn't happy with what we were doing at the time. Robert's new songs were more of a personal statement – entirely personal to him – and I couldn't make that statement on his behalf.' Matters worsened during the course of their cross-country trek with Siouxsie and the Banshees beginning at the end of August and which was scheduled to run through September and into October.

The idea of touring the UK with a band they admired was naturally a very exciting one, especially since they were treated as special guests rather than merely a support act, having been specifically chosen for the tour following a chance meeting between Smith and Steve Severin. They did have Chris Parry as a common denominator, Parry having signed the Banshees to Polydor. Relations between the two groups were cordial with Siouxsie even providing backing vocals for 'I'm Cold', the B-side to the third Cure single, 'Jumping Someone Else's Train', an attack on the current mod revival and the bandwagoneers who had hitched themselves to this rising star. A Smith composition that allowed the other two Cures little freedom for expression, it marked the end of the first phase of the band's evolution. Michael Dempsey couldn't accept Smith's desire to strip away everything but the very core of the song, and Robert took this as the final proof that he and Dempsey were no longer compatible. If proof of Robert's determination to plough his own furrow to the exclusion of all else were required, it came in an *NME* interview where he discussed the new material, pointing out that 'both lyrically and musically it's more fragmented, I can't quite define it . . . I'm intent simply on being able to do something that satisfies me.'

Personal problems were exacerbated by the intense nature of touring which threw the three together for twenty-four hours a day. As is so often the case, however, it was an incident beyond the control of the principals involved that hammered the final nail into the coffin. Just two shows into the tour, it was the Banshees not the Cure who disintegrated. Following a heated argument between Severin and Siouxsie on one side and guitarist John McKay and drummer Kenny Morris on the other at a chaotic signing session in an Aberdeen record shop, McKay and Morris jumped ship hours before the band were set to go on stage. Filling in desperately, the Cure played their normal set followed by some new songs that they were preparing for their second album, songs with which Dempsey in particular was very unhappy. Finally, to appease a restless crowd, Siouxsie and Severin came on stage to explain the situation to the crowd who were then entertained by a one-off version of 'The Lord's Prayer' with the Cure acting as backing group.

Following such a disaster, the tour was called off for a few days to allow the Banshees the time to regroup and it was during this period that the Cure recorded 'Jumping Someone Else's Train'. Both Robert and Lol offered their services as temporary Banshees, Robert getting the nod after the Banshees had already lined-up drummer Budgie, formerly with the Slits. The tour re-convened on 18 September with a show in Leicester and Smith gained plaudits all around for the impressive way he handled his slightly schizophrenic role of playing with two very different bands.

The greatest difficulties came away from the stage as Robert found further distance being placed between himself and Michael. Wary of gaining a reputation as unreliable, in order that no future gigs should be jeopardized, the Banshees understandably insisted that Robert should travel with them at all times on their luxury coach while Lol and Michael had to continue travelling in Robert's old Maxi. It was a stark portrayal of the polarization between leader and group, one which fazed Lol far less than it did Michael. Lol was enjoying the fruits of this small success, was a fan of the Banshees and was happy to make the most of this unexpected bonus of touring the country while getting paid for it. Michael on the other hand was rather more morose, becoming increasingly annoyed by what he saw as Robert's greater commitment to the Banshees rather than the Cure. When this mood was allied to his growing disenchantment with Robert's new material, the final seeds were sown for the dissolution of the line-up, with Robert conceding that at times he was holding himself back during the Cure set so that he could give a good performance later.

Contemporary press comments illustrated the depths of Dempsey's displeasure as he said, 'I don't want people to think of [Lol] and I as the Bruce Foxton and Rick Buckler of the band,' an expression of distaste at the way the star machinery was concentrated almost exclusively on Robert to their detriment in the same way that the press had built up Paul Weller in the Jam. The division in the group also had the consequence of driving Robert to escape it by spending more and more time with the Banshees which, of course, had the effect of fuelling Dempsey's displeasure still further. With both men unable and unwilling to compromise, there was only one potential outcome.

Robert later ruminated on the reasons behind the problems that he and Michael had endured. 'It was three people who just met once a week to play for enjoyment and it just became like a job. I'd known Lol since I was six but not Michael and the differences were between him and me. The more it went on, the more unbearable it became. I found on the Banshees tour that I was enjoying it more playing with the Banshees than the Cure. That's what really made the decision. Lol felt the same way, Michael wasn't criticizing or joining in on any level. We were getting really sort of banal . . . there wasn't much point in carrying on.' Whether Lol was quite as distressed as Robert is open to some question as he recently told *Record Collector*: 'I like him [Michael] very, very much but playing in a band involves a lot of compromise, which isn't Michael's strong point. What I was concerned with at that time was that something good should come out of it.' This provides further evidence that if Robert was the mainspring of the band, it was often Lol, in the early days at least, who kept the group ticking over.

It is revealing and ironic that Robert should be disappointed Michael refused to join in with the new material. Since Smith was so absolutely determined to go his own way, the likelihood is that, presented with material that he did not enjoy and aware that overtures were likely to be made to Simon Gallup in the near future, Dempsey felt himself frozen out and unable to contribute, though it's clear that the personality differences would eventually have made it impossible for them to work together in a situation of such enforced closeness. It also reflects Smith's astonishing self-belief that he assumed any songs that he might come up with deserved respect and admiration – it appears that hurt pride was perhaps another factor in the ejection of Michael Dempsey from the band. By November, Dempsey was telling the press that he had been kicked out and was looking for another band – he finally found himself in another Fiction group, the Associates. Typical of Robert's rather sheepish manner of changing the band's line-up, he left it to Lol to telephone Michael and tell him he was no longer needed, after Robert had already invited Simon to join the Cure. Internally, things had clearly reached crisis point, so much so that the blood-letting that came about with the loss of Dempsey was an absolutely essential piece of surgery bearing in mind that Robert confessed, 'At one stage I demanded certain things of Chris which I knew were impossible just to have an excuse to go, but there's a responsibility on me because I know that if I stop, the Cure stops.'

If the troubled relationship with Michael Dempsey was playing on Robert's mind during the course of the Banshees tour, there were other forces which combined to upset his equilibrium too, though ultimately it was these forces that were to provide the impetus for the Cure's second album, *Seventeen Seconds*. The major catalyst came in Newcastle when Smith found himself embroiled in a fight at the Cure's hotel. Over the course of that night Smith wrote the majority of the lyrics that found their way onto that record, but it was the process of touring itself that he found the most debilitating both physically and mentally, threatening his life away from the group.

Still engaged in a long-term relationship with girlfriend Mary Poole, Smith found that the periods he spent on tour were having a serious effect on their life together. 'If I wasn't in love,' he admitted candidly to *Sounds'* Phil Sutcliffe, 'being in a group would be an ideal existence but for me it's getting more and more difficult, really schizophrenic. To function at all, I have to keep the being in love completely separate from the Cure otherwise I would lose perspective and get sucked into the rock 'n' roll syndrome. On the road, I close down my emotions . . . *Seventeen Seconds* was written at the end of the Banshees tour, there were so many emotional wrecks walking around, so many things were awful in the group and at home, often I would have been perfectly happy to leave the group . . . so many times I've seemed to have a choice between keeping Mary or keeping the group,' an admission that if Robert had no doubts about the future, Mary did not entirely share that belief. Lol understood Robert's dilemma, sharing the same difficulties, agreeing that, 'There are two categories of you and they're battling against each other. If you value what you've got, it's a case of being totally celibate half the time.'

Later Smith was to admit that it was partially a desire to prove Mary wrong that drove him on towards success with the Cure and to turning it into a viable proposition, though Smith has always had the sense to divide his time between work and domestic life as evenly and fairly as possible. Nowadays, with his financial security assured, Smith seems to be one of the few 'rock stars' with the intelligence to enjoy his wealth and good fortune, spacing out his working commitments such that he only makes records or goes on tour when he feels the desire or the need to do so. Inevitably, however, as is the case with virtually any successful band you might care to name, the earliest days had to be dedicated whole-heartedly to the success of that venture. So great are the barriers to achieving long-term acceptance, it is only absolute concentration on the task in hand that gives any group the opportunity to succeed. That ruthlessness means that often people get hurt in the rush – Michael was an early casualty but so too, in different ways, were Robert and Lol and their girlfriends and family. All things were subservient to the Cure and in *Seventeen Seconds*, Robert seemed determined to expose that side of him, a darker, more sinister side than had hitherto been shown, confirming later that 'I desperately wanted people to see the ugliness in me'.

Taking the horrors that had assailed him in Newcastle a month earlier, at the conclusion of the Banshees tour Robert returned to his parents' home and began to write some new music which would complement the lyrics that he'd prepared. The bulk of this new material was written and demoed within a week using a Hammond organ, drum machine and his old Top 20 guitar – interestingly, he played the demos to Lol and Michael before Michael had been officially ejected from the group and his dismissive reaction, which sharply contrasted with Lol's enthusiasm, hardened Robert's resolve to boot him out. Smith had written this new material on the organ and wondered how the material could be transferred to a live setting, but the solution may well have already been in mind. Simon's group, the Magspies, had a keyboard player, Matthieu Hartley, another reasonably well-known figure in the Crawley locale whom Robert had come into contact with previously. Robert invited Matthieu to join the band not because of any desperate musical requirement, but to protect Simon. Feeling that Simon might be resented by others in the Magspies and therefore by many of those with whom Robert and Simon regularly came into contact, he chose to ask Matthieu to join to deflect some of the heat from Simon on both a local and national level. Hartley's simplistic musical approach was a nice bonus, though it was made apparent that he was maybe a rung lower within the Cure's hierarchy, as he admitted that basically he simply did what Robert told him to do.

The new four-piece group was also satisfying on another level. By completely changing the face of the band and adding an additional instrument, Robert had successfully reinvented the Cure and readied the band for their experiments in another musical idiom. With so fundamental a restructuring of the group, the press and public were aware that the second Cure album would be very different in both sound and character from its predecessor and so would hopefully approach it with few preconceptions.

More gratifyingly still, Robert had now been able to stamp his pre-eminence on Chris Parry and Fiction in much the same way that he had done within the group following the departure of Porl Thompson. Parry was close to Dempsey and had seen the Cure as being very much in the tradition of the great pop trios such as the Jam and the Police that were doing such good business at the time. His vision of the Cure was of them churning out great pop singles and building their fortune in that manner. Robert on the other hand knew that that was just exactly what he didn't want to do. He knew the sort of music that he wanted to make, the musical statement that excited and interested him, understood that it was liable to be less commercial a venture but dismissed such mundane considerations from his mind: 'I write songs for myself, it's very narrow-minded.' The vision that he had for *Seventeen Seconds* could only be brought into being if Smith was solely at the reins. Robert's sure-footed handling of the personnel change and the brilliant clarity of his perception of what the group could go on to do overcame Parry's initial reservations about the new songs. He had come to see that Robert would not allow anyone else to control his destiny and that he'd better let him get on with it. When the time came to record *Seventeen Seconds*, Chris Parry was no longer in the picture for Robert had decided he would produce the record himself with the technical assistance of Mike Hedges.

Chapter Six

THERE were touring commitments to honour before the new line-up were able to begin working on their first album together but this served as a useful musical getting-to-know-you exercise while on a purely personal level Robert was much happier with the situation, later suggesting that 'when Simon joined, it was the first time that I thought the group could go on and do something'. November and December saw the group playing a low-key British tour and then finishing the pre-Christmas period in Europe. Work continued on Robert's new material, the whole band contributing to the themes that he had determined, shaping it for the recording sessions that were due to commence at Willesden's Morgan Studios in January 1980.

Writing continued in the studio in a fairly idiosyncratic way as Simon noted. 'When we record, if it's still not right, it means everyone sitting around Chris Parry's kitchen [Parry's office was near the studio] all night scrawling sheets and sheets of paper. For "At Night" we got really desperate and finished up at six in the morning with Lol standing on the table pressing his head against the ceiling because he thought that might help.'

Lol's role as peacemaker and bridge-builder within the group was taking a new turn by this stage as he became the central victim or scapegoat within the group. Matthieu commented, 'Dear old Lol, he's the master. We beat him up, wind him up, frame him up but he understands. He knows we have to release our tensions in some way and he's the target.' What started out in a fairly light-hearted vein was to have more serious consequences for Tolhurst as the years went by. However, Matthieu's comments did illustrate that there was a nasty undercurrent of violence that was rarely far from the surface of the group; in suggesting alternative ways of life for his band-mates, Matthieu stated that Simon's favoured existence would involve having inflatable wimps chained to his leg so that he could kick them at will. The Cure, while at times clearly a great source of enjoyment and fulfilment for the quartet, was also a band with a darker side. Robert also confessed, 'I've always written things down . . . mainly because I get really angry and I've got a really violent temper but it's not physical because I don't think I should vent my frustrations and depressions on anybody else.' This was an assertion that foundered on the 'Pornography' tour when Smith, in keeping with everyone else in the entourage, became physically violent.

That pent-up aggression found its way into the new album for although the spirit of the band had improved immeasurably with its new recruits, the same horrors of his dependency on the group and on touring racked Smith's mind and seeped into *Seventeen Seconds*. Recording itself was spread over a week, mixing taking a further week in February. The approach was clearly far more measured this time. Having achieved a modicum of success they were granted a little more studio time to look for the effects they wanted while the delicate nature of much of the material demanded that greater care be taken. Oddly perhaps, given the desolate quality of a lot of the finished product, the sessions were conducted in good spirits, all four still enthusiastic about the band's new line-up and the exciting possibilities that stretched before them as they experimented with a different style of music. Their approach to recording was new for them too as they worked through the night and slept in the studio, a method that was to persist through Cure history.

Though Robert had fairly defined ideas about the mood of the record and the emotions that he wanted his lyrics to convey, he would regularly alter them throughout the recording sessions, not committing himself to a finished version until they were finally sung to his satisfaction. To a degree, the lyrics were almost incidental for the atmosphere was vividly captured by the musical content, music which conveyed a sense of loss, of dislocation and of regret. Against this evocative backing track, Smith's lyrics were far less precise than on *Three Imaginary Boys* though there were exceptions to that rule. Generally, however, he seemed reluctant to reveal too much of himself to any outsiders though those around him would inevitably have a far greater idea as to what he was driving at. 'I do it for myself, I'm trying to communicate with myself,' was Smith's explanation for what others perceived as lyrical obscurity.

Seventeen Seconds was a brave attempt to reflect on different aspects of the same emotion, a variety of moods rather than themes. Robert recalled its intense genesis in Newcastle for his erstwhile *bête noire* Paul Morley in *NME*: 'It was a really condensed incident, a rush of feelings that I'd found in myself had been watered down, mainly by playing in a group. It's a really strange situation, but I find touring and things like that shut me down. I harden and get very reclusive, sort of shun people. I'm not naturally an extrovert person but sometimes I get really withdrawn and it irritates people . . . it's just something that happened, all the things that I'd been shutting down just came out in a big rush and for the following two weeks, every day I'd just be thinking about that particular incident. One day I'd wake up wanting to kill somebody, the next day I wouldn't even bother getting up. It was awful, I was letting myself slip in order to write songs. I wasn't fighting it, whereas in everyday life you have to control those feelings. It was a really demented two weeks.'

Smith being so heavily affected by one incident that it could completely unbalance him for weeks on end calls to mind an earlier comment in the group's life when he was fending off criticism that the Cure came from comfortable middle-class backgrounds and thus knew nothing of real life or struggle. Vehement in his denial of such an accusation, Robert quite sensibly hit back, asking, 'Why do you have to be born in poverty to know what's going on? Quite often I think it's the other way round. If you don't have to fight for your existence every day you can maybe take more time out to think.' Always careful to steer clear of pretension in interviews, he showed that he grasped the fine line he was treading when he admitted, 'I do take myself seriously but there's a point beyond which you become a comic figure.' Smith's music has nevertheless always been informed by his interest in deeper questions of life and love, his fascination with just how he fits in to the greater scheme of things, and with his feelings of the overwhelming futility of life. As time went on, his lack of any religious faith or belief in any life or existence beyond death became the central theme of much of his songwriting though early on he was worried 'that my words aren't going to interest people because they're mainly about me, how I feel, they're not about world situations and alternatives'.

Rather than mouthing fashionable political platitudes à la The Clash, for instance, Smith was keen to dig deep within himself to try to reconcile his disparate emotions and the different facets of himself which were at war with one another. *Seventeen Seconds* was the first real step in that direction as it spoke with real spite, immense vitriol at times, and hinted at a very deep sense of self-loathing as well as an over-riding belief in the sanctity and validity of his choice of lifestyle.

Yet Smith's lyrical outlook has changed little in the fifteen years since *Seventeen Seconds* was recorded. As recently as 1993, he admitted, 'I think I know less than I did when I was a teenager . . . the same things still worry me. I still see an utter pointlessness to everything in my bleaker moments. I don't think it gets better with age . . . you're forced to close down as you get older because you can't break down and cry on the factory floor because either you're a nutter or a nonce or something. You just can't do it, but I think it's that pressure that forces people to give up . . . when you're a teenager you're still able to express that kind of emotion and not feel embarrassed by it . . . I know that I'm not living in the nominal "real world" but even if I wasn't doing this I would still be around people that I could feel like that with. To me that's the idea of growing old, no longer being able to say what you really feel, always having to pretend that you feel something else.'

That attitude had a large role to play in suggesting the direction of *Seventeen Seconds* for Robert recalled that period as being a time when 'we were all realizing that we were no longer young', although in fact he was only twenty at the time. External pressures and responsibilities were being brought to bear on the group, long-term touring and recording plans were laid by record companies and this was something against which Smith felt very strongly. When that was grafted on to personal problems inflicted on him by the very nature of life in a group, especially on the road, the resulting music had, of necessity, to be dark and emotionally extreme.

Taking a look at Smith's lyrics which, by Michael Dempsey's testimony, were becoming more and more personal and self-obsessed, the central motif of *Seventeen Seconds* was his changing relationship with Mary as the Cure began to take more and more of his attention, a situation he encouraged yet abhorred. The group itself was becoming almost incestuous in its refusal to acknowledge the outside world, Simon saying that, 'I don't think there's a better band or better friends. Our girlfriends get jealous because if we're split up for four days, we miss each other.' Such commitment is scarcely the greatest foundation for maintaining a relationship away from the group, particularly when that relationship is inevitably part-time because of touring requirements.

Rock 'n' roll folklore suggests that life on the road is rarely the most sober of existences and so the strains put on the personal life of each individual Cure and their respective girlfriends is obvious. Robert's lyrics deftly reflected the spectrum of opinion within the group seen through his own very personal perspective. 'In Your House' was an important piece of the whole jigsaw and Smith said of the song, 'It's about uncertainty in love, our knowledge that what we are doing is destroying our personal lives . . . you keep saying, "Oh, we'll just do this tour, go to America and then it'll be alright." But if it falls flat then you can be left with nothing and always be bitter about it. It can destroy your life.'

'In Your House' was a song which underwent significant changes during its evolution. Again, the *Curiosity* collection on the tape of *Concert* provides a useful indication of the territory that *Seventeen Seconds* was exploring and just how quickly it was changing since its version of 'In Your House' was recorded in Holland while the band took a brief break in the midst of the album sessions and the song sports a completely different set of lyrics. Whether those which made it on to *Seventeen Seconds* were an improvement is a matter of personal taste – the live version was possibly more explicit, certainly a bitter take on the song, while the studio version was more despondent, more desolate, filled with something approaching despair.

The despairing mood which permeated the rest of the record was most marked perhaps on the instrumental sections like 'A Reflection' or 'The Final Sound' while 'Three', with echoes of Pink Floyd, was a soundtrack to a mental breakdown. Infidelity and what Smith saw as the temptations lying in wait for a touring group and the hollow nature of that experience compared with life at home appeared to be high on the agenda as songs like 'A Forest' seemed to suggest. Smith wasn't slow to attack himself either on 'M', which sounded like a conversation between the two halves of his personality, Robert Smith and Robert Smith of the Cure; it was a disturbing attack on what he felt he was becoming.

The most startling impression that *Seventeen Seconds* gave was that Smith was determined to spare neither his own feelings nor those of the people close to him – 'Play For Today' was an obvious instance with its wanton display of selfishness and simultaneous berating of those that would stand in his way or hold him back. Later, in talking to *Lime Lizard* magazine, Robert admitted that Mary 'gave me ultimatums in the first three years, it was either her or the Cure . . .

she would never have stopped me because I made the choice of the group and said "you're coming along as well" and eventually she did because she wanted to . . . she thought I was going to waste my time when I could be doing something else and I had to make her see that it was what I wanted to do. So that's why it was important whether we got anywhere or not . . . she admitted that she wished we were not going to do well so that I could spend all my time at home.' The striking thing in such a statement is the combination of Smith's suggested guilt at his treatment of Mary and yet his absolute determination to do precisely what he wanted to do whatever the consequences. It's a testament to the unusually strong relationship they share that it has endured despite Robert's refusal to compromise in those early years of the Cure.

Perhaps more than any other factor, this selfish streak explains why the Cure are so popular – their audience surely recognize aspects of themselves in Smith's contempt for all but himself and would love to follow that path but are unable to do so, forced into the compromises that the 'real world' requires. Smith and the Cure allow that audience to live vicariously, to escape and occupy a space where self-centredness is not only acceptable but positively encouraged. That audience, which is a regenerative and perpetually young one, is one that sympathizes with Smith's refusal to 'grow up', to accept limitations or to compromise. It's a pure attitude insofar as it is not tainted by the moral hypocrisy of age and the need to fit in. 'I felt I was grown up at the age of thirteen,' Smith asserts. 'I haven't learned anything more since. I've faced the real world and denied it. As a group we retain our childishness in that we get excited, we ignore obstacles and we go for things in a determined childlike way. And I think that's good . . . I still despair when I look at the conventional world of adulthood.' It may not always make Smith ideal company, but it does make him strangely honest.

The title track seemed a little different to much of the preceding material in its effective deployment of a disconsolate guitar line while Smith sounded close to tears as he mourned the loss of his youth. More reflective, the Cure seemed to be suggesting that their own demise might not be too far away, Robert ruminating further on the way in which his dream of a life within the group might elude him while simultaneously regretting the passing of time and lost, forgotten memories.

Smith's obsessive worrying over the passing of time is fundamental to his writing. If he has been described as living within a hedonistic whirl at times, then it's also true to say that a different part of his life is controlled by his anhedonic urges, in that he is unable to enjoy the present since it is so fleeting a moment, a time that will soon be taken from him: 'Sometimes I can't bear the thought that I'm doing something, some little unimportant thing and I won't be able to remember it.' His songwriting drive is partially explained by his need to trap memories and moments, to write them down so that he can continually refer back to them. As a madman expecting the apocalypse stocks up on tinned food, Smith hoards emotions and experiences, his songs functioning as the cupboards where he keeps them.

On studying its subject matter – and the caveat that Smith's writing was already becoming so heavily coded that external interpretation is a tricky business – it would be hard to find a less personable or amiable album than *Seventeen Seconds*, but it would be equally difficult to find a more assured and confident one, amazingly so from a group still so inexperienced. Smith's despair at the passing of time, his perennial dismay that he's running out of time, and that that renders all else meaningless, transformed the group into a far superior unit than the one that had knocked out *Three Imaginary Boys* a year earlier. *Seventeen Seconds* firmly fixed the Cure in position alongside Joy Division and Echo and the Bunnymen as the doyens of miserable rock, helping them quickly find a fan-base and a pigeonhole which would ultimately restrict the band, Nick Kent calling it 'depressingly regressive'.

Oddly for such a downbeat collection, *Seventeen Seconds* provided the Cure with their first hit when 'A Forest' crashed into the charts at No. 31, earning them their first *Top of the Pops* slot, for which they were required to fly back from an American tour. Naturally for so independently minded a group, the idea of *Top of the Pops* was greeted with very mixed feelings indeed. It was obviously a relief to have sold sufficient records to get on the programme in the first place, particularly in the light of Robert's fears about the consequences of failure and the need to sell records in order to feel that they were grabbing attention, yet *Top of the Pops* itself represented so much of what the Cure resented and hated about the music business – it showcased all the inane rubbish that had caused the band to start up in the first place. In spite of Parry's urgings, Robert was initially determined that they should not do the show. Significantly it was Simon who finally changed his mind, significant in that it illustrated the growing self-reliance of the quartet.

'I didn't want to do it,' recalled Robert. 'We were trying to succeed without it but Simon said if we didn't do it, somebody else would and that you couldn't change anything if no one knew who we were. I came to see that we had to get a certain level of exposure because you can't present a choice unless people know a choice exists.' Having agreed finally to do the show, the experience itself was a severe chore, the sort of work that Robert had always attempted to reject, matters being worsened by a hand injury that Robert had suffered while trying to change a tyre on their van in America. Their performance was stone-faced and uninterested, though Robert defended himself later, arguing that, 'You have to be bored with it. You either have to be so desperate for success that you're willing to put up with being treated like an idiot or you react in one of two ways – boredom or you just get drunk because there's so much sitting around.'

Releasing 'A Forest' as a single was an astute move, its nagging melody and bass line recalling '10.15 Saturday Night' and providing an easy way into the new album, a painless introduction to a completely different Cure, a transition signalled by the album's artwork, a series of blurred images – Robert had taken charge of this facet of Cure operations too, though he did retain the services of Bill Smith to help him achieve the required effect. As a consequence of the success of 'A Forest', *Seventeen Seconds* found its way to No. 20 in the album charts, an encouraging progression from their debut, particularly given the less easily digestible music the band had created this time. With such success came the inevitable calls to go on to the live circuit and so the band dived head-first into a rush of concerts around the UK and abroad.

The schedule they had to fulfil was, to say the least, back-breaking. Initially, the new line-up took the strain quite well, all revelling in the excitement of doing something new as a unit, even if Robert's was the controlling voice. Matthieu expanded on the theme, telling *Sounds*: '[Robert] does have the most say on things, but that's fine because to my mind he's the most capable. He handles the lot – all the financial side from our point of view.' However, the Cure being the Cure, all was not to stay rosy for too long, and as had been the case with Michael Dempsey, their intensive live schedule soon brought to the fore personality differences, a situation not helped any by the ridiculous amount of trouble the group found themselves in – arrested for public indecency in Holland, getting lost en route to concerts, having their van impounded and being involved in a riot which necessitated the use of tear-gas at a festival in France.

The relationship which was most fraught was that between Matthieu and Robert, Matthieu often expressing himself violently, Robert recalling their partnership as 'physically the most volatile. Me, Matthieu and Simon used to fight a bit, drunk, rolling around the floor in bars' while Matthieu's short fuse saw him hurling his synthesizer into the crowd in Germany. Part of the difficulty stemmed from the way in which he had been conscripted into the band in the first place, as an afterthought to placate locals who might have resented Simon leaving the Magspies. Being a keyboard player in a band that didn't especially need one was not the easiest job in the world and once the novelty began to wear off, Hartley soon grew frustrated with his lack of involvement within the group's structure. Things came to a head during a month long tour of Australia and New Zealand which grew in size and intensity as the band packed clubs everywhere and were forced to do extra shows to accommodate demand eventually playing almost every night. Matthieu and Robert became involved in a fight that led to them leaving their hotel and making the newspapers for Who-like excess. Hartley became completely estranged from the group, spending his free time alone.

Musical frustration was at the heart of the matter as the keyboard-player understandably wanted to expand his role. Just as Dempsey had found himself restricted by Smith's musical requirements, Matthieu found that his tastes and those of the group's leader rarely converged. Work that he felt augmented the songs was treated as an abomination by Robert who was still determined to weed out any form of musical excess, desperate that each song should be a model of economy with no superfluous embellishment. At the same time, Matthieu felt that Smith was leading the Cure into a musical dead-end, staking out territory that Joy Division had already looked into. The suicide of Ian Curtis just after the release of *Seventeen Seconds* illustrated perfectly the dangers and the unhealthy nature of a morbid fascination with death and depression and Hartley wanted none of it. Meanwhile, the press were looking to cast Smith in Curtis's role, penning the Cure into that area of music from which there might be no escape. Hartley did not share Robert's obsessions and didn't grasp what Smith was looking to do – Smith's declaration that 'if I'm going to write songs I want them to be about something that matters to me' meant Hartley felt excluded and could no longer stand firm as part of the group, disappointed that the admittedly lop-sided democracy seemed to have ceased to function. Finally, he decided that he wanted no further part in the Cure story and left the band on their return from Australia. Had he not jumped, he would surely have been pushed, but his decision at least meant there were few hard feelings.

Robert meanwhile was engaged in the live hard and play hard syndrome, aided and abetted by Simon and Lol. The Cure were embarking on something of a crusade, keen that the records and live performances should have the same intensity as the original emotions that Robert was writing about. Playing up the anonymity angle that he had been so upset with when shown the *Three Imaginary Boys* artwork, the Cure now proudly boasted of relegating the idea of 'image' to its rightful secondary position, proclaiming that it was only the music that was important, not some tasteless sales gimmick. The repercussions of that crusading attitude were to shape the next phase of the Cure, and their fervour to lead to its ultimate destruction.

Chapter Seven

MATTHIEU'S accusation that the Cure were going down a dark route was certainly true. Robert was going through a particularly sombre spell in his own life which had to feed into the music. He had begun a period of questioning everything about himself the year previously, a process that had informed and inspired *Seventeen Seconds*, in which his uncertainty expressed itself in sadness or in anger. Having given vent to his reactions to himself as songwriter and quasi-rock star on a personal level, he now moved on to questions of faith both in its religious context and as a means of asking himself if he was following the right path.

Over the years, Robert has insisted that *Faith* was initially conceived as a positive record, an answer almost to its predecessor. Circumstances prevented its realization in that form, turning it into an altogether darker collection. Early attempts at demoing new material in September 1980 ended in total failure as the group were unable to create the sound Robert was chasing and the sessions quickly gave way to further live shows where some of the new material was worked upon. It wasn't until the new year that the band tried again by which time the emphasis had changed from positive to a kind of existential desperation. The original plan for *Faith* had been to explore the concept of faith on different levels and from different standpoints, a similar concept to *Seventeen Seconds* but with different subject matter.

However, by the time recording was to begin in February 1981, Lol's mother had become terminally ill and Robert's grandmother had died. The two were devastated by these personal tragedies and they were forced to re-evaluate what it was they were doing. Robert found himself suddenly struck by his absolute lack of anything approaching religious faith, a total absence of belief in anything beyond the here and now, a frightening realization. The inevitable conclusion to that line of thinking for him was to think that everything was ultimately rendered futile, pointless. For Smith and Tolhurst, raised as Catholics with all the indoctrination that that implies, coming to terms with the situation was particularly difficult.

Smith had already thrown himself into the subject, visiting churches, watching the congregation and attempting to make some kind of sense of people living their lives in the service of a hereafter that, as far as he was concerned, did not exist. If he could comprehend the complete absurdity of making records and fretting over the smallest details within that process, that was far less ludicrous than following a God that did not exist, submerging all your own drives and desires and ambition to His greater glory. Even so, Smith's investigations, which led him to write songs in churches, must have left him with a very uncomfortable feeling – at least the true believers had something that made sense of their lives while he, who could not empathize with their beliefs, was lost. If they were living a life of self-delusion, it was at least a comfortable one which provided a peace of mind that Robert himself could not approach even by following his own instincts.

He confessed to *Q* in 1987, 'I feel dreadfully lonely sometimes. It's the worst feeling in the world and it's partly because I have no faith. I no longer believe in my own soul.' Going on to talk about 'If Only Tonight We Could Sleep' from that year's *Kiss Me Kiss Me Kiss Me* album, he noted: 'In that song I'm harking back, wishing I could still believe in my guardian angel, but I know I'm just wanting something that's gone for ever.' The strong Catholic strain to pronouncements such as that suggest that losing his religion was a painful, difficult business.

To one with his background, religious study often goes hand in hand with fear – fear of damnation, the fear of the need to do penance for past sins, indeed the fear of God. For one so sensitive to his own faults, those fears must have lurked at the back of Robert's mind even given his total lack of belief, leading him into the unenviable paradox of an absolute disbelief in the redeeming aspects of religion, coupled with the recollection of his Catholic teaching that insists that sin demands atonement. The period of *Faith* was one in which Robert appeared to struggle to free himself from the last vestiges of his religious upbringing, for the preservation of his own sanity if for no other reason. Revealingly, he had told *NME*, 'I'm not doing this to make my name go down in history. I really couldn't care . . . I've got faith in what I'm doing from a personal point of view but as to whether I go down in history I'm very doubtful about that. If I let that worry me along with everything else I'd crack up before I'm going to anyway.'

Back as a trio again, the Cure had returned to the ideal set-up for the skeletal music they were attempting to produce. Keyboards had had a fairly peripheral role within the group and it made sense to allow Robert to flesh out the sound with guitar, with one or other of the band making the occasional foray with the synth during the set. In such a way, all three were fully occupied musically during a set and had little opportunity to become frustrated in the way Matthieu had previously.

It seemed painfully obvious that a trio was right for the group and that given the personalities involved there was a chance this Cure might last longer than previous incarnations. Robert and Simon were very close friends, while Lol remained generally easy-going, maintaining his role as court jester. This clique was jealously guarded by the three to the exclusion of all others, including Chris Parry who, shunned by the band, naturally began to lose interest in them.

For Robert, what the Cure should be attempting was very clear cut; he knew the music he wanted to make, how it should be made and how it should be presented. In Lol and Simon he had the ideal accomplices to help him achieve his aims and so he simply shut out everyone else, giving no one access. At the time, he noted, 'It would be impossible for someone else to fit into the Cure now really, because it's so insular it's untrue. It would take somebody about ten years to be accepted, I think, on the same level that we accept each other. It's like being married in a way.'

Parry was naturally disgruntled, labelling the three as 'incestuous' though much of that was Smith's doing. To make the records he wanted to make within the time span he had allowed himself, he felt it absolutely essential that the band be cocooned from outside distractions or influence. Additionally, it appears likely that Robert, particularly affected by his own loss, felt that only Lol and Simon could understand what he was going through since they were the closest people to him. Their music of the time seems to reject the outside world even more than had previously been the case. *Faith* was a record specifically compiled by the Cure for the Cure. To call it therapeutic would be misleading for there was no resolution within

Above: Robert takes a photograph to remind himself of band personnel. Simon, Lol, Matthieu and Robert in the mirror, 1980. (*Retna*)

Robert in unpadded cell shock. (*Ian McKell/Retna*)

Right: Robert has a bad hair day, 1986. (*Ross Marino/Retna*)

Left: Mary and Robert at the social event of the year, the BPI awards, February 1990. (*McGough/Pictorial Press*)

Above: Mary questions the value of Robert's magnetic personality, August 1989. (*Jennifer Rose/Retna*)

Below: Siouxsie Sioux anticipates the loss of another guitarist as Robert checks the exits, 1983. (*Pictorial Press*)

Lol and Robert, the Lovecats,
1983. (*Steve Rapport/Retna*)

Left: Robert has great expectations for X-FM, 1993. (*Chris Taylor/Retna*)

Above: Lol and Robert wonder who'll be next to go, 1983. (*Matthews/Retna*)

Below: Cure FM – Chris Parry, Robert and DJ Mike Halloran disturb London's airwaves, 31 August 1990. (*Randall/Retna*)

Tim Pope exolts the virtues of intensive mulching within a successful garden. 'I Want To Be A Tree', 1984. (*Tim Pope/Retna*)

Steve Severin and Siouxsie Sioux ponder the reliability of self-certification sick notes. (*David Tonge/Retna*)

Top band. Andy, Lol, Porl and Robert, 1983. (*Pictorial Press*)

Perry appreciates the fringe benefits of becoming a full-time Cure, Great Xpectations, 1993. (*Chris Taylor/Retna*)

Left: Five men having finished '1,000,000 Virgins'. No wonder they look tired. Back: Porl, Boris, Lol. Front: Robert, Simon, 1987. (*George Chin/Pictorial Press*)

Below: Barbershop quartet. Without the barber. Perry, Robert, Simon and Boris, 1993. (*Steve Double/Retna*)

Right: Lol and Robert attempt
to squeeze Michael out of the
picture, 1979. (*Paul
Slattery/Retna*)

Below: Just like heaven
at the MTV Video Awards.
Roger, Porl, Simon, Robert
and Boris, 1989. (*Pictorial Press*)

Right: It's never enough for Robert, 1990. (*Ronnie Randall/Retna*)

Below: Wishing impossible things. Porl, Perry, Simon, Boris and Robert, 1992. (*Neils Van Iperen/Retna*)

its songs but it did provide the outlet for the group to release some of the powerful emotions that they were struggling to cope with.

As a group they enjoyed one another's company and certainly didn't spend all their time in morose navel contemplation, but once others tried to invade their protective space the mood swiftly changed to one of resentment – contemporary TV and radio interviews show the group in confrontational mood. The crusade of which Smith had spoken had really begun by now, imposing a crushing intensity on the group under which they struggled to survive, occasional outbursts of violence breaking out as tensions built. The atmosphere became especially fraught as they entered the studio, for the music simply would not come. Despite moving from one studio to another with monotonous regularity in search of a sound or of inspiration, the band could not get the sounds that Robert wanted on to tape. Appropriately for the subject matter, Robert had imagined a funereal, stately pace for some of the songs, a feeling that was just beyond their grasp however often they tried to play the songs.

External influences beyond their strained emotions took their toll. The Cure had been on tour almost constantly ever since *Three Imaginary Boys* had been released two years previously and, in playing *Seventeen Seconds*, they had begun to perform music that was highly charged. By the time Matthieu left, the group were jaded and in need of a rest they didn't get, their punishing schedule doing nothing to alleviate the problem. Michael Hedges, again producing the album along with the Cure, had reached the point where he had nothing to prove while Robert had little with which to challenge him. The two parties knew one another too well to be able to fashion excitement from ground they'd already covered and if familiarity didn't breed contempt, it did breed lethargy, precisely what was not required in dealing with complex material that demanded absolute perfection from its atmospherics if it was to carry the necessary emotional weight.

The songs themselves did little to make life easy as the lyrics were literally dragged from Robert's fairly fragile spirit – *Melody Maker* suggested that they conjured up a spirit of 'defeated inertia', exactly Robert's state of mind at the time. In his demoralized defeat, the strain of working hard on finding the necessary vocabulary for songs that couldn't be pinned down was especially taxing and probably the last problem that he and the others wanted to tackle. Finally, by Chris Parry's testament, drugs were making themselves felt within the sessions as Robert sought to find inspiration and fresh energy from external sources, his own reserves severely depleted by his internal confusion.

In all, this cocktail of unfortunate circumstances could, perhaps should, have led to absolute disaster, even the breaking up of the group. However, the support they provided for one another was a crucial factor in helping them through the creation of *Faith*, thoroughly vindicating Robert's vision of the band as a collection of good friends rather than a collection of musicians who had little time for each other. If they were preoccupied with their own mortality and questions of faith, this inevitably only took up a percentage of their time as Robert later reflected for *Q* in 1993. 'I write very infrequently but when I do it's because I have to . . . when I'm writing songs, I am in the emotional state described . . . but I'm like that about 10 per cent of the time maybe.'

In February 1981, that 10 per cent was probably closer to 50 per cent for the mood of *Faith* was bleak, desperately sad. Robert eschewed any real guitar work of note, and Simon's bass took centre stage for much of the record, its deep resonant quality running through the album like a mournful heartbeat. It was a sign of just how much influence Smith had had over his playing that he was able to play in a restrained fashion tailor-made for the songs. 'I had to unlearn a lot of things,' Gallup said at the time, 'because I used to like playing eight notes a second or something but now I don't really care any more – I play a note a minute now.' Gallup's adaptability and desire to fit in with Robert's vision helped explain his longer tenure with the Cure when compared with Hartley or Dempsey, both characters unwilling to compromise.

If *Faith* had a failing it was that the Cure were not quite sufficiently experienced musicians to be able to fully realize Robert's concept – *Disintegration*, a record constructed from the same fiercely passionate mould eight years later was a superior model simply because by that time the Cure had a surer grasp of what they could and couldn't do. At times on *Faith* the group faltered, although in fairness this was partially because of the chaotic conditions in which the album was recorded. Robert at one point gave up singing out of despair at the direction the sessions were taking, and began to scribble lyrics on the studio floor, before Parry stepped in to attempt to give the recordings some shape.

Robert surprisingly conceded that the tracks were recorded in a very dispassionate manner, which gave them an odd, detached quality, at their best somehow ageless in keeping with church music. As a seamless whole, *Faith* embraced a ceremonial richness, a processional feel that served the lyrics well – the juxtaposition of the religious-sounding music and the hollowed out, spiritually defeated lyrics was striking in the extreme. Robert Smith on this record was a lost soul shrieking from the edge of a personal abyss – that these were songs torn from his heart was beyond question.

The first glimpse that the Cure granted of this private world was with 'Primary', a song that had something of 'A Forest' about it. While Robert's anguished vocal made it clear that this was no perky little pop tune, it was still the most commercial offering on the album, propelled along by a pounding bassline, eventually making its way onto the singles chart and providing them with another thrilling opportunity to go on *Top of the Pops* during which they again refused to display any interest in the proceedings. The single came in a sleeve designed by Porl Thompson who had approached Robert to inform him that he could improve on their previous work. With fellow student Undy Vella, Porl formed Parched Art and took over the production of virtually all Cure artwork thereafter. Having been a member of the band in previous incarnations, Porl had a natural affinity with Robert and was happy to absorb the music prior to producing any artwork, so that he could get a feel for precisely what mood Robert was trying to convey. This collaboration was an important first step towards breaking away from their anti-image stance and producing a recognizable Cure identity.

Like 'A Forest' before it, 'Primary' didn't really prepare people for the parent LP but it did perform the crucial task of getting them to buy the album and give it a chance. The single came out after the album but its presence in the charts produced a healthy boost to sales, *Faith* placing at No. 14. 'Primary' was, to an extent, harking back to *Seventeen Seconds* in its regret at the passage of time and the belief that age simply leads to a closing down of emotion, a switching off of feelings that ultimately leads to the breakdown of relationships. The suppression or denial of honest emotion as people grow older has become Smith's perennial topic and is clearly something that he fears might afflict him in the future. There was a subtle difference with 'Primary' in that it was a far more resigned piece than anything from the previous record, revealing an understanding that innocence does not prevail and a desperation that things cannot stay the same.

Intimations of his own mortality were central to *Faith*, an obvious progression from his acceptance that he was no longer physically young. He told *Lime Lizard* later that, 'I am afraid of death and romanticizing it is a way of accepting it . . . I think ultimately it's a pretty depressing subject unless you have a total belief in the afterlife.' The stately opening of 'The Funeral Party' provided the ideal environment for the group to broach that subject but in a hesitant fashion as if Smith was aware that he was breaking all our cultural taboos by daring to discuss the notion of death, and making the song an impressionistic rather than a directly affecting one for outside listeners. By contrast, the brooding, menacing 'The Holy Hour' struck a direct chord with its stark imagery of a man desperately wanting to believe, to feel comforted by the promise of salvation yet finally accepting that he has no faith, and railing at the self-deluded way in which others grab blindly for some promise that will allow them to make sense of their lives.

Smith appears incapable of accepting that others do genuinely believe in life after death and in God, seemingly dismissing it as hypocritical self-deception. The acceptance that whatever he might do with his life, whatever nominal sins he might commit, there would be no penance to be extracted by a vengeful God was to have direct repercussions for the behaviour of the Cure over the next eighteen months.

The music on *Faith* had a hypnotic quality to it, brought about by Robert's fascination with Indian mantras and Benedictine chants and this repetition gave further ground to the idea that this was a semi-religious record, some taking it as evidence that Smith was affirming his religious beliefs when the opposite was clearly true. On 'Other Voices' a dispirited bass figure formed the central core, Robert wailing a lyric that expressed a kind of universal angst, a heartfelt scream of anguish against the loneliness that could consume him even within a city of eight million people.

The only piece of aggression to interrupt *Faith*'s musically serene progression was 'Doubt'. It was peculiar that this should be the only passionately played track given that Cure shows of the time were transformed by the powerful intent that the group displayed on stage yet here it was as though the subject matter and the studio problems had drained them of any heart, giving the music a lack-lustre edge that served to accentuate Robert's impassioned vocals on this track still further. Whether by accident or design, that musical reserve produced the right environment for *Faith* which closed with the cornerstone title track.

Smith's difficulties with his lack of belief and the effect that had on his mental state persisted far beyond the recording of the album, but it was with that record that he made steps to address the issue. The title track itself remains one of the most affecting songs that the Cure have produced in their time together and it still provides a stunning climax to their more intense live shows. It is not a song that is inevitably played as part of some placatory greatest hits package but is only employed on nights when Robert feels able to perform it within the correct emotional setting. It is a feature of Cure shows – a feature that makes them possibly the most powerful live group in the world on one of their best nights – that the whole group throw themselves into performance with absolute abandon. As the focal point of the show, responsibility broadly lies with Robert himself and, in recognizing that in the traditional role of frontman he is something of a disaster, Robert instead promotes his feelings and emotional ideas. More than any other song, 'Faith' provides that opportunity and on nights when Smith is particularly affected by his surroundings, or when his personal demons are fighting for control, he will completely change the song's lyrics to fit the mood. The performance is at times mournful, sometimes distressing, often physically frightening, and to see Smith put so much of himself into it dispels any doubts as to his sincerity and also raises questions as to whether he could ever finally quit the stage altogether since it palpably brings out the very best in him.

Faith as it stands on record reflects his tortuous, relentless pursuit of perfection, of ideal, idealized moments, someone to say the right thing at the right time. The final conclusion is that there is no sanctuary for him within religious ritual, life consequently being senseless. The hollow nature of the whole record, the emptiness that is the inevitable consequence of a quest unfulfilled, a search that confirms only negatives, culminates in 'Faith' where Smith recognizes that only temporary solace can ever be gained, and even then only from within. The faith that's left at the end is a faith in himself and in what he is doing, an escape and yet also an immersion into the philosophical questions that trouble him. Smith seems to want to put the questions behind him, to go on and live his life without this self-inflicted torment but has no idea how to free himself, leaving the album on a note of utter desolation rather than the positive, life-affirming mood that self-belief should bestow.

Criticism abounded that the Cure were making a living from the propagation of dismal sixth-form poetry and monotonous dirges and there was something in such reviews – Smith's lyrics were deliberately obscure or, more accurately, he had no intention of widening their scope to allow others to look more clearly into his mind. What the critics couldn't accept was that *Faith* was never constructed with any audience in mind but with a complete disregard for anyone beyond the sessions. Ray Lowrie dismissed the record as 'grammar school angst' in *NME*. Smith's emotion, while not expressed in a manner in which it could be linked to real incidents within his life, was a real emotion, overwrought perhaps, but a genuine expression of grief and confusion, of futility and defeat. The concerts that preceded the album's release and those that followed it showed very vividly that Smith was living through these songs, that he was trying to find his way through these traumatic experiences and sensations. Robert Smith was truly a lost soul trying to come to terms with that situation as best he could. If that excluded other people, that was a price he was more than willing to pay.

Partly in keeping with the control-mania he was displaying at the time and partly as a sop to those who wanted evidence that the Cure hadn't completely lost their sense of humour, they hit upon the idea that rather than take a support group on the road with them, they would take a film instead. Robert explained at the time that the idea of using a support group was unfair all round in that they often had little or no time to soundcheck which in turn meant that they would sound terrible with neither group nor audience enjoying the experience. From the Cure's point of view, the concept of having total control of the entire concert was seductive – they were able to control the music that played over the PA system as people came in, they could show a film that was in keeping with the music, provide the soundtrack for it themselves and then play their set, thereby maintaining a tight rein over the evening's atmosphere.

Originally, they approached film schools and colleges to provide film makers there with an opportunity and the finance to make a film that would be seen by thousands of people but were disappointed by the reaction, explaining to John Gill in *Sounds*: 'There was no commitment . . . they were very jaded. There was no real enthusiasm, they were very cool about it.' Such lack of interest when faced with such a great opportunity was one of the cardinal sins in the Cure canon for while they were labelled as fatalistic, cynical mopers, their naive excitement over for new ideas and experiences had been retained and was effectively their reason for carrying on.

Eventually, Ric Gallup came to the rescue by producing a hand animated film, entitled *Carnage Visors*. He was an abstract model maker, and made use of that skill as the film was based around a small figure twisting and turning in a thousand ways as various indiscernible shapes passed behind it. When the tour began, the film was incomplete, Gallup having filmed it originally with incorrect light settings which meant that once it was processed, it came out completely black. The film that the group took out with them was shot in three days of frantic work, Robert defending the film by saying, 'It's really, really basic . . . for a film it's very naive. But it works on that level. I think it needs slightly more contrast just to hold people's attention,' a problem that was addressed by the gradual editing in of additional footage. 'It will become a series of pictures,' Smith added, continuing, 'A lot of the processes used are like ballet.'

The idea of using film was not a new one to the band, Robert noting that, 'The idea to have a film was there when we were making *Seventeen Seconds*. People often think you're being self-indulgent when groups talk about making films but there's a lot of ideas that spill over from making records . . . the Cure is a reflection of our lives, it seems stupid just to limit it to music.'

The obvious film medium for a pop group was that of the promotional video and the group had of course been hounded into making these for their singles, all of which had been uniformly awful with the band expressing no more interest in them than they had in *Top of the Pops*, an odd attitude from a group so keen to control their own affairs. Part of their lack of interest could be explained by Robert's dislike of artifice as he admitted at the time. 'We don't present shows . . . we could contrive to make it visual and everything but we're not like that naturally so why should we?' *Carnage Visors* was a middle ground between the two, a visual exploration of the

Cure's style of music which simultaneously refused to be drawn into the stereotypical wacky pop group madness on which the standard music films and videos were based.

The idea of *Carnage Visors* was both engaging and entertaining but its use had ulterior motives for the group. Firstly, it provided Robert with the opportunity to develop a musical idea without the traditional constraints that would have been placed on him within a normal album situation and so he was able to experiment further with repetitious music that evolved gradually over time. The piece was composed within one evening using an out of tune bass guitar and a rhythm box and provided an evocative soundscape but one which could never have found a home other than as a soundtrack composition. Perhaps more importantly, however, the screening of *Carnage Visors* prior to the Cure taking the stage acted as a useful barometer of the audience. Where they paid scant attention to the film or jeered while it was showing, the band would take to the stage in belligerent mood playing their most aggressive shows as they took the attack to the crowd, while at shows where the audience had shown interest in the film, the music was emotionally intense in a different manner, more reflective and in keeping with the original concept of *Faith*.

Crowd disturbances were not the only problems that they faced, however, for relations within the group were starting to turn sour once more as the Cure began to implode. Taking *Faith* on the road in this way as the 'Picture Tour' was quickly revealed as an awful decision for the dense, claustrophobic atmosphere of gloom that the music created had a deep effect on everyone within the troupe, casting a pall that was difficult to dislodge. Similarly, cracks were appearing between Robert and Simon following the sessions where Robert had often found himself trying to prepare himself to sing these introspective, powerfully, painfully emotional songs while Simon and Lol were in the control room getting drunk. Grudges of this sort didn't seem to last between Lol and Robert, possibly because of their shared history, but Simon was still a relative newcomer to the band despite his long association with Robert and, since both had fairly volatile temperaments, under stress things could often become difficult.

The final straw came when, while playing abroad, news reached them of the death of Lol's mother, a crushing blow that brought home to them the reality of death as opposed to the more abstract concept they were dealing with. Given the prevailing mood that lurched from hedonistic fun to grim despair, it's reasonable to suggest that there was a disturbing lack of equilibrium within the group. Lol insisted that the tour continue as a way of coping with his loss but the Cure had by now set themselves on a downward spiral from which there was little prospect of escape. The next phase of their development showed just how far down that road they had gone.

Chapter Eight

I F THE 'Picture Tour' was demanding, somehow the group still managed to find time to record a new single. Maintaining the ethic of releasing no more than one single from an album – a principle to which many impoverished collectors might wish they still adhered – demands for a new record from Polydor and Fiction meant that a new song had to be put together. Based on the book of the same name, 'Charlotte Sometimes' was the offering they chose to record, doing so in mid-July 1981, again with the assistance of Mike Hedges, the final time they were to work together. Sounding like something of a leftover from the musical era that *Faith* represented, it was mannered and lethargic, lacking the impact of earlier material while the B-side, 'Splintered In Her Head' was far more interesting, signposting very clearly the way ahead for the Cure.

Harder and harsher, with a splash of real venom in the playing, the song revolved around an almost tribal rhythm. It had an underlying current of viciousness to it that intimated that Robert and the rest were tiring of the never-ending whirl of work and were capable only of an aggressive reaction, something quickly illustrated by their response to audiences who wouldn't accept the atmospherics of *Faith*, Robert and Simon frequently jumping into the crowd for a fist fight. Their American tour in the early summer had also been turbulent, Robert on occasion not having a clue where he was or why he was there.

The 'Picture Tour' took the band through to the end of November and bingeing was high on the agenda. They indulged in all manner of sensory delights. Later Robert remarked that, over this period, he and Simon had a 'good go' at killing themselves, though whether this is a comment to be taken literally or simply an observation made in hindsight based upon their lifestyles is a question that perhaps even they cannot answer.

However, it's not hard to make some obvious connections based upon the Cure's musical progression. *Faith* was part of a process of questioning, a process which left Robert flat – and the record exuded a dejected air of resignation. The next record would inevitably have to be a reaction to that. But why should there be another record? When you've subjected yourself to a thorough process of introspective questioning only to conclude that there is no point, why not give up? Is there any sense in getting out of bed, any sense in trying to create further records when everything is rendered aimless? When the very concept of life itself becomes a hopelessly surreal one, why bother? Robert's answer was simple. 'I had two choices at the time which were either completely giving in or making a record and getting it out of me. And I'm glad I chose to make the record. It's really the key action of my life, making that record. It would have been very easy just to curl up and disappear.'

Robert might easily have crawled underneath a rock after *Faith* had it not been for the intensive tours to which he had already committed himself, for if he'd rejected Catholicism, he was seemingly imbued with the Protestant work ethic and had no intention of cancelling the tours. The very act that kept him going was however also the source of further disorientation and grief as the demoralized songs they were performing night after night seeped into him. Initially a burst of drinking and/or drugging might be dismissed as typical rock 'n' roll fare, a simple safety valve to relieve the tensions of a heavy workload. The Cure's hedonism was far more than an occasional isolated burst but a daily occurrence and as such can only be construed as a symptom rather than a cure.

Numerous possibilities suggest themselves in trying to rationalize their behaviour, the first being that there is no rational explanation in what, if their previous records were any guide, they regarded as an irrational world. Where all is nonsensical, what do the actions of a few people matter? Going further than that, if Smith could find nothing that might give him a belief in anything beyond the present and his own life, and given that his selfish streak had been the propulsion behind the group it's hard to see him accepting the existence or importance of anything beyond his immediate circle. What licence would that grant him? It's not beyond the realms of possibility to suggest that given his agnosticism, he was finally released from the concept of penance which in turn freed him from acting within any kind of moral framework – the only sanction that might enter his thinking might be the danger of courting Mary's disapproval or falling foul of the forces of law and order.

The concept of morality was something that gave Smith food for thought, for much of *Pornography* was to address itself to the concept of moral hypocrisy and his own personal conflicts. The sonic density that was achieved on the record was a potent backdrop to Smith's preoccupations and gave the whole thing an oppressive air from which there was no prospect of escape. Robert had compiled the drum tracks himself having borrowed Lol's kit during a brief break in touring and the patterns he constructed created the illusion of suffocation, Robert's voice calling for help and trying to break free of the music, a reasonable allegory of his attitude towards the Cure at that point.

His lyrics of the time suggest that his behaviour was sometimes wild when away from home, yet he had not freed himself from the consequences and appeared racked with guilt over his indiscretions, yet seemingly unable or unwilling to help himself overcome them. In a sense, this is the natural reaction to an absence of faith. If on consideration life cannot be given any rational shape, if it has no meaning beyond this moment then its futility can be an overwhelming sensation, one that could torment every waking moment if it were allowed to. As people throw themselves into drugs and drink to forget painful personal events, then so might Smith have added to his list of personal woes this utter depression that rendered everything point-less. To blot out that feeling might be the only possible method of carrying on with life for to spend every moment in contemplation of such issues would be intolerable – that way lies madness.

There is also something of the self delusion within such sybaritic rites. Was Smith trying to convince himself of his lack of faith and his rejection of Catholic teaching? By taking a check-list of all the vices proscribed by the Church and systematically working his way through it, Smith's defiance in the face of God and religion could be construed as a final act of contempt.

Smith recalled that during the *Faith* tour, 'We lived this doomy semi-religious record. We sort of wore it everywhere we went; it was like sackcloth and ashes . . . it wasn't a very enjoyable year, really.' By the end of that run, Robert had grown tired of the Cure and of the whole rock 'n' roll lifestyle but had yet to formulate a means of escape. Financially, the band were compelled to go through dense periods of touring simply because they had an expensive show with a large PA, lights and film equipment but were playing to small audiences for small return. To remain financially viable, they had to tour but, in turn, this was affecting their own lives and their reason. Robert was suddenly struck by the conclusion that he had spent far more time in the company of Lol and Simon than he had in that of Mary and knew that he had to redress the balance. To his absence was added the guilt associated with his lifestyle, all of which seeped into his lyrics and attitude. He was left to wonder, 'How could anyone put up with what Mary has to put up with and still like me as much as she does? She must have a capacity for liking me that goes far beyond anything else and I don't feel as though I deserve it a lot of the time.' Smith was well aware of his unacceptable side, saying, 'I've been monstrous at times . . . just generally being horrible. There is a desire in me to destroy things, you can say I'm quite destructive. Things that I actually like I feel uneasy about, I feel uneasy about being comfortable.'

Seemingly worried by the fragility of his own mind, Robert turned his attention to reading books about mental health and the treatment of people in care. Reflecting later, he pointed out, 'If it wasn't for Mary and if I hadn't had the family that I do, the upbringing and the credentials that I've got, I would have got myself committed a couple of times, because you just give up. Some people do.' Out of this grew Smith's commitment to Mencap as a charity, to whom both he and the Cure as a group contribute. Although people have often come to dismiss him as a woolly thinker incapable of precision, Smith's summing up of the problem of mental health care is wholly accurate and extremely perceptive, recognizing that because some people do not carry the mark of disability, be it crutches, a wheelchair or whatever, they are not considered disabled, yet mental illness can be the most debilitating form of disability. The alternative is often treatment of the 'pull yourself together' variety towards which Smith takes an understandable dislike, angry at the simplistic treatment of a malady that can taken an infinite number of complex forms. Others can be termed mentally ill simply because they do not share society's imposed values.

'I feel that the people who are truly mentally handicapped are a sort of forgotten minority. Quite often people who are classified as mentally handicapped aren't at all; there's so many levels to it. And yet they're just pushed out of the way a lot of the time. It's not an obvious disability in some of the forms that it takes but there's a complete lack of sympathy for them, not just in this country but world-wide . . . I think there is good reason why these people should be taken care of. The whole problem is that everyone is lumped together as being mentally handicapped and shoved to one side; nothing's really ever done for them.'

Through 1981, Robert had been pushing himself to the extremes, Simon and to a lesser extent Lol taking part in the ride. In addition to the possibilities already outlined, it seems that Robert chose to drive himself to the brink of a breakdown, partly from internal problems that he couldn't resolve and partly out of a desire to see how far he could go and whether it would aid his writing. 'I just wanted to see what it would feel like, the whole thing of reaching a chronic physical and mental decline through obsession.' His drug intake inevitably left him in a dangerously unbalanced state from time to time and reading his lyrics for *Pornography* it's clear that he was living through all kinds of delusions at that stage. It's a variation on the perennial trap for musicians who begin to use external agents to fuel their creativity only to find that in the end they are the ones being controlled. Robert later admitted that he couldn't remember great chunks of the *Pornography* sessions while those around recall him being out of his head but simultaneously fighting for control. 'There was a different intensity, a belligerence about [that period]. We didn't actually care if it was making us go mad in the process, we had to do it,' Smith later remembered. 'The reasons for being in a group at that point had reached extreme degrees. I was on a crusade – a very drug-induced crusade – against myself and everything else that was going on.'

Everything that surrounded *Pornography* conspired to create a truly savage environment. Robert went away on his own following the final *Faith* shows in Britain in December 1981, locking himself away in Windmill Studios in Surrey to demo this new material. Once he had laid down some basic ideas, Lol and Simon joined him but this was a radical departure from the way the Cure had operated before – if Robert had previously been the ringmaster, this time he owned the circus, preventing any kind of artistic collaboration. He knew what he wanted and demanded that the others follow the party line which they were reasonably content to do, the demos being completed within a week, leaving Robert satisfied.

By now it was the turn of his relationship with Simon to go sour. The British tour just completed had seen 1313, featuring Steve Severin and Lydia Lunch, as one of the support groups. Happy to rekindle his friendship with Severin after his spell with the Banshees, Robert spent a great deal of time in his company which upset Simon who felt that *he* was Robert's main confidant. However, this internecine jealousy was not one-sided for Simon had a very large personal following within the Cure's audience and so, recalling Robert's earlier attitude towards Porl the guitar hero, Robert may well have been less than delighted with Simon's popularity which could prove threatening to his pre-eminence within the group.

The relationship between Simon and Robert is an odd one, Robert comparing it in some ways with his relationship with Mary while Simon has regularly adopted an almost protective role towards Smith. In hindsight, Simon was willing to accept all the blame for the breakdown in communications between himself and Robert around this time but this seems to be an inaccurate, if tremendously loyal, piece of self-sacrifice. Chris Parry's view of the situation was that Simon was left out in the cold simply because Robert was going through the introspective search detailed already, at which point his selfish streak came to the fore, and he had little or no time to interest himself in the worries of anyone else. Parry was upset with the turn things were taking, seeing that it might spell the end of the group, later explaining that, 'Smith himself admits that he was going through a particularly bad patch . . . being inspired by certain aspects of mental illness in addition to personal problems. At that time, the band were reasonably perverse, so it wasn't a façade as some suggest.'

Gallup had given himself completely to the Cure, saying that, 'It's 99 per cent of things really – friends. That's all you need, besides the 1 per cent which is the drink!' Gallup believed in the gang mentality of the band, a group of friends setting sail against the world but for Robert the Cure had become something more. When they finally came to record the new album, from January to April 1982, there was a repeat of the problems which arose during *Faith* where Simon would spend his time drinking – partly a function of Robert using him as little more than a session player which left him plenty of time to kill – while Robert was desperately trying to capture the necessary intensity for his vocal, while battling with his personal problems and trying to maintain a certain detachment so that he would be able to fulfil his duties as co-producer, something which would have caused him both regret and impatience with his band mates. Lol and Simon consumed so much alcohol they were able to construct a mountain of beer cans in the corner of the studio to which they would retreat when necessary. Over the period of recording, Robert's paranoia plumbed new depths which made him resentful of everyone and everything. 'I just hated everything around me for about a year,' he later agreed. Simon naturally felt somewhat detached from the ferocity of Robert's very deep-seated personal crisis and felt bitter that his friend did not come to him for help but sought solace in the company of Steve Severin instead. What for Robert was a necessary change of scene, stimuli and company was for Simon a grievous blow.

Robert had hooked up with Steve Severin prior to Christmas 1981 just after the *Pornography* demos had been completed in Surrey. He spent a brief period staying at Severin's flat during which time, by his own account, he wandered around London hallucinating in the course of what was later termed a 'chemical vacation'. Under Severin's protective gaze, Smith set about writing the lyrics for *Pornography* in his addled state, a revelation which explains the dense incomprehensibility of much of the imagery on the record. *Pornography* succeeds in the same way that *Faith* did, by virtue of its musical potency but lyrically, while revealing and therapeutic for Robert himself, it's mostly an impenetrable wall of words with the occasional hole through which you can just catch a glimpse of Robert's ideas.

Phil Thornalley was an unusual choice as producer given his previous track record with Duran Duran and the Thompson Twins and at first he and Robert failed to hit it off but, as time went on, Thornalley proved his worth, helping Robert find the clarity of individual sounds so necessary given the overall density which *Pornography* required. The opening track, 'One Hundred Years' was a case in point, probably the most successful piece on the album in its combination of music and lyrics as Robert launched into a diatribe against moral hypocrisy, asking the central question that was inevitable in the aftermath of *Faith*; 'How do people cope?' Seeking to understand how people could manage to live in a world devoid of meaning, Smith tried to look into the world of business, the world of the nine to five, of ambition and hope, alien concepts to one who viewed the world through carnage visors and who felt that it was a surreal, futile little planet that rendered such abstract concepts as those ludicrous.

To open the record, Smith placed one of his best lyrics at the head, an expression of the futility of existence. 'The first line on *Pornography* . . . there could be nothing more throwaway than that. To me, that's a really funny line – I really think that! I'm as convinced by arguments for the end of the world as I am for saving whales – it's a completely theoretical area. If I saw someone jumping on a baby I'd probably go over and try to stop them but, at the same time, I can sit here and glibly say that it doesn't matter if we all die.' Aware that the Cure were currying favour from those who turn depression into a way of life, a fashion accessory to flaunt, Robert knew the effect such a lyric would have and used it to great effect, almost as a comedy feed line. It was to be the last laugh on the record.

Given the way it was recorded, it would be surprising indeed had *Pornography* become a barrel of laughs, for apart from the personal antagonism that existed between Smith and Gallup, Smith was becoming increasingly isolated. For the duration of the record, the band lived at Fiction's offices, sleeping rough, Robert erecting himself a kind of tent where he would hoard assorted possessions like a jealous hermit. Fiction effectively closed down over that period for Robert had reached such a state that he could not tolerate intrusions from anyone outside his immediate circle. Evidently, even there, communication was poor, to the extent that Simon partly misunderstood the concept behind the record, suggesting that it should be called *Sex* not *Pornography*. The point that Smith was making with the title was that it was not the material itself that was inherently pornographic but people's reactions to it, from where the principle could be extended to people's negative attitude towards the disabled, the mentally ill or the disadvantaged. From there it's a small step to applying the term to moral hypocrites who live within the sort of self-delusions that *Faith* had addressed, or who immerse themselves in the world of commerce as though it offered salvation. Smith did not spare himself either as some of the more explicit lyrics prove.

Of 'Siamese Twins', Smith now says, 'It's like re-reading diaries. That period, I tend not to dwell on too much because it wasn't much fun.' That song, which he described as being about love's uglier side, along with 'Pornography' and 'The Figurehead', offered brief insight into a deeply trouble psyche, what *Record Collector* described as 'his frantic attempts to reconcile his Jekyll and Hyde morality'. Yet *Pornography* as an album was not as frantic as it might have been nor as Robert would have wanted it to be. The record was book-ended with belligerent aural assaults of diverse natures with 'One Hundred Years' and 'Pornography' but between them Smith's masochistic fury seemed to have dissipated, as though gaining the experience had drained him of the energy to turn them into the biting music that he wanted. Later he would say that *Pornography* was made about 'the inability to be violent', addressing the Cure themselves, unable to break free of the confines that surrounded them but also at people in the wider world who could not shake off convention.

Unwilling to go into further detail about the record, Robert evaded the issue by saying, 'There's really no answers or solutions to anything we've done,' adding, 'I don't expect to be told things in songs or have something illuminated for me . . . it communicates, but nothing specific, just the desire not to feel isolated.' These explanations sounded more like a palatable way to excuse his failure to create the precise impact he was aiming for and, in more candid moments, he did concede his disappointment. 'You develop certain ideas and follow them through in the hope that you're gonna mean something to a certain section of the population. I don't think we've ever really achieved it. If I'd watched the Cure or bought Cure records, I know, being honest, that they wouldn't mean what I was hoping they'd mean . . . it's a case that the ideas have always been strong enough but the execution of them hasn't been.'

Yet the Cure had assembled a fiercely devoted following, and this was part of the problem which besieged Robert. 'It's worrying that people have built a need in themselves for someone like me. If it wasn't me it would be someone else . . . I hate the idea that you'd die for your audience and I was rapidly becoming enmeshed in that around the time of *Pornography*, the idea that Ian Curtis had gone first and I was soon to follow . . . I think a lot of people around me at the time seemed to enjoy seeing me in that state. It's tragic to try and continue to live in that sort of mode because people who do that just end up surrounded by people who feed off the notion that they're living on the edge. In fact they're the most conservative, dull, drug and alcohol-ridden people. I'm glad I did it when I was young enough to recover physically.'

Smith had obviously reached the end of his tether by the time *Pornography* was released to negative reviews – Dave McCullough's

NME review called it 'musical crap' – but a healthy chart placing at No. 8. The attitude of the press hardened Smith's convictions that he was right – the final lines of *Pornography*, which had opened with its nod towards futility, saw Robert Smith seeking a cure and determined to fight for the right to the rest of his life. Before he could decide what form that fight would take, he and the band had to endure 'Fourteen Explicit Moments' on the road.

Chris Parry had already expressed reservations about *Pornography* as a record but, having to book a tour, put things in motion, though this time dates were scheduled only for Europe and the UK. Attempting to make the concerts into a show to add some life to what he saw as difficult music, Parry introduced the idea of film screens. More importantly for their future, Robert began to use make-up quite extensively in order to create an impression, his first real effort to fashion some sort of image around himself. 'On that tour, we used to wear lipstick around our eyes so as we would sweat it looked like your eyes and mouth were bleeding. It made my eyes sore so I stopped that but I liked the pictures of me with a really gashed mouth because I haven't got very pronounced features and it helps me to pretend I'm not me.' That last admission was to prove central to the later progression of the Cure, but the idea of having bleeding eyes and mouth shows just how savage things were becoming and how much self-loathing was involved.

Given the internal disintegration of the Cure, it would have been a surprise had the tour passed off untroubled. The music they were playing had intensified, leaving Robert mentally drained after each show while Lol recalls that the audiences in Europe were very small despite the larger halls they were playing, a response guaranteed to drive Smith further back into his shell. With just a couple of weeks left of the tour of Europe, the skirmishes that had been breaking out intermittently within the band and their crew finally exploded in a night club in Strasbourg when Simon hit Robert, leading to an all-out fight. Both left the group immediately though, after three days' cooling off, they resumed and completed the tour. Once the tour was over, the Cure was effectively dissolved.

Intense music often treads a fine line between true feeling and simple doom-laden self-indulgence but the knowledge of the group's impending demise did help them walk that tightrope. Robert accepted as much, noting, 'On the tour when everyone realized it was going to be the end of the Cure as a band, for about five days it became really violent for the first time. It reached the point when we came off stage, everyone was completely empty.'

Pornography was the culmination of a well-planned undertaking which had left the Cure, particularly Robert, drained as it reached its natural conclusion. 'The Cure's evolution follows what I'm like. *Three Imaginary Boys* is very naive, we were really young when those songs were written, then *Seventeen Seconds* and *Faith* are really uncertain and *Pornography* is quite violent . . . After *Three Imaginary Boys* which I hated straight away, to pull off a three-year project like *Seventeen Seconds* to *Pornography*, I realized we couldn't be seen to do it in a half-hearted way, so we threw ourselves into a whole lifestyle that was a vicious circle . . . By *Pornography* we weren't having any fun and it seemed pointless, because by then we were only doing it for other people and it all fell apart . . . everyone involved in that tour disintegrated somehow, their characters became distended. They seemed to revert back to something horrible inside them, and there was a lot of physical violence. We just took our lives up on to the stage. It was a distressing time and it made me go quite odd for about eighteen months . . . it all got too intense and depressing, everything was wrong, we were stagnating, me and Simon were fighting and we hadn't got anywhere. I was very proud of *Pornography* but no one else liked it . . . I thought the group would just stop.'

Simon's response was similar, though again he tried to take the greater share of the blame. 'We recorded *Pornography* which was a bit intense to make and then toured for twelve weeks playing those songs and meaning them. It was hard not to go a bit funny and I think we all did but it showed more in me. It was best that I went for a while because I didn't laugh any more.' Robert took issue, admitting that, 'I wasn't very good fun. That's why the group broke up, because I'd reached the point where I couldn't bear anyone to be around me, basically.'

Other factors had their say in tearing down the Cure, as Robert explained. 'Things had become too structured and we were obligated to do too much. One of the ways out of that was that if it became not a group, then we would be under no obligation to do anything.' Turning up to play the same places year in year out can be a pretty deflating business and that lack of fresh stimuli had driven the Cure to the edge. Having made *Pornography* and lived it for three years, where could the Cure possibly go? Gallup had offered a suggestion that indicated the void that had opened up between him and Smith:

'Simon had a particular idea of what we should do next, something even more grizzly and inaccessible to all but a few. I just saw it as a dead end.'

It was obvious that Smith needed an outlet for his talents and frustrations. 'The group is there to escape the oppressiveness, it's a way of screaming,' he said, and so he clearly had to devise a method of working in the future. 'We had to do something ludicrous.'

Chapter Nine

'ON *PORNOGRAPHY*, all I could do was fucking howl and cry . . . it was about things that have far-reaching effects, far more concerned about some of the horrors that people go through just in everyday living . . . the year I did *Pornography*, Mary couldn't even bear to be with me.' Once affairs had reached this kind of crisis point, Smith knew that something had to be done to escape the trap. He admitted, 'I would just give up if I couldn't communicate with Mary,' and since *Pornography* had illustrated that he wasn't yet ready to give up, his lifestyle and attitudes had to alter. He added, 'I wanted to get away from myself as this morose and deeply tortured person. I found that really stressful.'

That level of stress left Smith with only one option, which he gladly grabbed. 'I just felt really stale and took a break, and in that sense the Cure doesn't exist really. It has got to a point where I don't fancy working in that format again . . . I was getting really sick of being surrounded by the same people all the time.' Further distancing himself from the group, he said, 'It's not like being in a band any more, when there was a kind of unity involved. I still have a passion for the ideas that we come up with and with what we actually do but not in the sense of being in the band. I would now feel as much passion for something I did outside the Cure as inside the Cure. To me now, it's just a specific medium.'

Although he had wrapped up the Cure for the foreseeable future, he was still writing songs while away on holiday. The pressures of the last few years were not eradicated simply by taking a break and Robert spent the next couple of years in a state of what might best be described as 'personal confusion' trying to free himself of that frenetic madness and its legacy. It became very clear in August 1982 that Simon was no longer part of his plans when he recorded a song for

Flexipop magazine. 'Lament' was billed as being by the Cure, but the personnel this time was Robert and Steve Severin. The two were looking for an opportunity to work together, something prohibited by Smith's work with the Cure and Severin's commitment to the Banshees, though they regularly socialized together: 'I used to go out with Severin a lot to dance clubs but we wouldn't dance. It'd be more like take drugs and try and get to the toilet which would usually take about two hours . . . we became good friends but we were never very good for each other. Our friendship was based entirely on altered states. Whenever we went out together I would never come home until the next day. Mary hated it.' In fact it was to be the Banshees that were to cement this new partnership as they had succeeded in losing another guitarist, John McGeoch, who had collapsed with nervous exhaustion. Robert accepted the offer of the post, initially as a temporary member before quickly assuming a position as full-time Banshee, immediately embarking on a tour of Europe with them in November.

Smith's acceptance of the opportunity of going on the road was interesting given that it was partly his antipathy towards touring that had fuelled the Cure's spiralling internal decline – the aftermath of *Pornography* saw him issue the first of his regular threats to give up touring altogether. At various points in the early years of the group, he had said that playing live was the main reason for him being in a group and that even had the Cure failed, he would have continued to play in pubs. Of course, with the Banshees, the pressure was very much less than with the Cure. 'The Banshees thing came along and I thought it would be a good escape as I was getting fed up with things . . . I was really disillusioned and decided to see how another group operated.'

Sioux was the very public face of the Banshees and the one the TV, press and fans wanted to talk to and the internal hierarchy of the group meant that it could be no other way. That being the case, Robert was given the chance just to play music again with no other considerations to bother him – essentially it was, to employ the golden cliché, a back to the roots exercise, insofar as it allowed him to recapture the enjoyment and excitement of playing guitar, to relive just what it was that had inspired him initially. 'I joined the Banshees to get away from being the front person in a group and performing more obviously for people, because Sioux does all that,' he said. Similarly, it reduced some of the personal pressures on him to come up with a new viable direction – rumour had it that with his defection to the Banshees, the Cure would be no more. It was a rumour he was happy to encourage since he could then buy additional time to come to grips with what he wanted to do next.

Not only did Siouxsie and the Banshees provide Robert with time away, they also allowed him physically to leave the country, something that Robert was rather pleased to be able to do in November, for in that month a new Cure single was released by Fiction. 'Let's Go To Bed' came about through the urgings of Chris Parry as an attempt to ensure that the Cure did not go down without a fight. Robert had already expressed considerable dissatisfaction with everything that they had come to represent. Talking to *ZigZag*, he said, 'I worry that the Cure do not have enough impact, not in the sense of popularity because that's never concerned me, but in the sense of what we mean as a concrete idea . . . I always want to shatter any complacency. We tried on *Pornography* and somewhere it worked. The track "One Hundred Years", that was a real departure and we wanted that atmosphere throughout but somehow it got diluted. The very image that the Cure conjures up lacks impact, the drab/grey wastebin.'

In an interview with *Melody Maker* he suggested that 'there were far too many things working against [us] really; things of our own making like the anti-image and all that rubbish. Instead of trying to get rid of that at an early stage, we flirted with it so there was nothing to latch onto. I realize now that was probably a big mistake, not establishing ourselves as personalities earlier on.' Suggesting the solution, he added, 'Having a hit single can work – recognition through that success might mean that people are intrigued and that's a good thing – giving a band the chance to start afresh with a new audience even if the interest is facile. The records sell, but the problem is they are selling to the same people and that can dull the hope of breaking out. It's not really commercialism – I wouldn't mind diminishing the volume of audience if it meant achieving something more definite.'

Dismissing the single later he concluded, '"Let's Go To Bed" is probably the only contrived record we'll ever make because it was designed to break the mould of what the Cure had become, which I thought was very static and stagnant so I wanted to attract a new audience and make everybody young again.' The last point was central to the Cure's philosophy of recapturing a sense of excitement, of wonder and of innocence coupled with a dogged refusal to admit to any limitations. Harking back to Simon's confession of the fragile state of his own mind post *Pornography*, Robert's summing up was simple. 'I went peculiar, but I got out of it with "Let's Go To Bed".'

Parry's view was that the best way of tearing down the old Cure was to do something completely atypical, as far removed from *Pornography* as possible. Having picked up on the Cure back in 1978 when they were still dabbling with pop songs such as 'Boys Don't Cry', Parry felt that it would be refreshing for Robert to try to recapture that side of his songwriting while for himself, as owner of Fiction Records, he would not look askance at the idea of a hit single. Robert was clearly intrigued by the possibility, particularly once it was suggested to him that perhaps he couldn't write that way any more. Goaded into response, he came up with 'Let's Go To Bed'. 'I just wanted to see if I could write a really dumb pop song that would get played on the radio because I hadn't written anything like that for ages and ages,' he explained. Further justifying this departure he said, 'I tried to break the mould of the Cure because I knew I'd want to do it again but not from where we left off with *Pornography*.'

The single was recorded in October 1982 with Robert and Lol convening without Simon. Simon in fact had no idea that the Cure were working again, ousted in the same way that Porl had been years before. Simon was actually staying at the Fiction offices and answered a call from a fan who wanted to know what studio Robert and Lol were working in! Though he had never been told, Simon now joined the expansive ranks of ex-Cures – Robert's view was that since he was the clearly acknowledged leader of the band and that he and Simon had so clearly grown apart, it was up to Simon to have the courage to leave, though he was so wrapped up in his own world that he didn't really care either way. Put simply, their friendship had deteriorated through a combination of outside influences and their own personal determination to do things their own way. Pride prevented either from approaching the other to sort matters out and things ended in bitterness all round. Whatever the rights and wrongs, Smith and Gallup were to steer clear of one another for a further eighteen months, a move that was undoubtedly beneficial to the physical and mental health of both.

The 'Let's Go To Bed' sessions threw a further spanner in the works, one that was to have wide-ranging implications for the future of the band. Robert had created what he felt was a 'horrible sounding' dance record that incorporated every disco cliché that came to mind including a syncopated drumbeat. Here, stories began to diverge. Robert's version is that, 'When we did "Let's Go To Bed", [Lol] tried to do the drumbeat for it for about three days and it cost us a fortune in studio time. In the end we got in a session drummer [Steve Goulding]. He was going to pretend he played it, until I pointed out to him that if he had to play it somewhere and couldn't, he'd be humiliated.' Smith also contends that: 'I did [the single] on my own and Lol was just there for company, basically. I was spending late nights in the studio and he was just someone who'd sit there and I'd talk to.'

Lol's version is somewhat different, in that he suggests that he had already tired of drumming prior to the sessions, realizing that there were technical barriers that as a self-taught drummer he could not overcome without considerable study. At this point, he chose to move on to keyboards, giving weight to Robert's contention that, drums apart, he himself was the sole contributor to the single, since it is unlikely that Lol would have had time to become sufficiently proficient prior to the recording taking place.

Nevertheless, Lol was making attempts to remain a useful member of the Cure, taking piano lessons in London. 'I went to see a little old lady in Maida Vale, who looked like Miss Haversham. She was three-and-a-half feet high. She had two baby grands in her basement flat and she'd slap me on the back of the hands if I got anything wrong,' which in terms of punishment sounds like a breeze compared with some of the more blood-curdling acts of alleged victimization perpetrated on him by the Cure. It's easy to under-estimate his role over the first four records when such strong characters as Robert and Simon were involved but, even now, there's little dispute that his role as class clown and then increasingly as scapegoat helped keep the group together. Robert dismisses that aspect of their history, noting that 'the one characteristic Lol has had is that he likes to be liked at all costs', though given the bitter legal battle that raged between Tolhurst on one side and Smith and Fiction on the other in 1994, it is inevitable that a degree of spite and self-justification should creep in to any discussions of the past. Even so, Lol did survive all the upheavals of the early years of the Cure, coming through periods when Robert might just as easily have put together an entirely different line-up without him. Smith now puts this down, tongue-in-cheek, to his own 'angelic compassion' but in

1983, Lol described their relationship more fully. 'It worked out that only me and Robert really get on with each other permanently . . . we don't take each other seriously. There's always something that brings us back, it's like a shared history.' In more charitable times, Robert described Lol as 'like an old blanket, very threadbare and dirty and you don't think why you're carrying it about until you realize you couldn't throw it away because you're emotionally attached through mutual experience.'

Just as crucial to his tenure was his level of eagerness to remain in the group and belief in what they were doing, Robert accepting that, 'I must be hard to work with over a period of time. I suppose that people just get fed up with that single-mindedness.' Where Matthieu and Michael had been less willing to compromise, Lol understood Smith's drive to realize his vision and was perfectly content in the subordinate role of helping him, whatever the context. There was a certain detachment between the two also which might help to explain the longevity of their friendship. Smith and Gallup had such a close relationship that, particularly bearing in mind their youth and the pressures that encroached on them, it was almost bound to founder at some stage, if only temporarily. The relationship between Smith and Tolhurst was less intense and so less prone to breakdown.

All in all, 'Let's Go To Bed' was an extremely eventful recording for it also successfully soured relations between Smith and Parry to the point at which Parry threatened to sue Smith who responded by threatening to break his legs. Having made the record, Smith felt it so out of keeping with everything that the Cure had ever done that he got a severe case of cold feet and refused to allow its release under that name, feeling that it would taint the band with something unpleasant as well as disappointing the fans. He suggested that it be marketed as a Robert Smith solo record or sold as Recur, but Parry vetoed his appeal and demanded its release, certain of its potential as a hit single and similarly convinced of the long-term good it would do Robert and the future of the Cure. Smith's response was to strike a bet with Parry – if the single wasn't a Top Twenty hit, Smith would be released to do something out of contract. According to Smith, Parry agreed but, when the single peaked at No. 44, tried to renege on the agreement, taking legal action to prevent Robert joining the Banshees.

Having worked with Smith for five years, one might have thought that Parry would have realized that trying to coerce him into a course of action was precisely the wrong way to go about things. Parry must have felt his hand forced, which was clear evidence that, despite this semi-sabbatical, all was still not entirely well with Robert and the future of the Cure far from certain. If Robert knew what he was going to do, and that seems highly unlikely, he certainly wasn't saying.

Yet 'Let's Go To Bed' was the start of an association more successful and enduring than any other in Cure history: with Tim Pope, video-maker. It's difficult to argue with Smith's analysis that the Cure were a group condemned to dismissal as gothic drabs – their foolishness and sense of humour had rarely come across. Yet Smith was surprised at people's lack of any historical perspective: '"Let's Go To Bed" was deliberately wacky and it shook people's idea of the group which was strange for me to accept seeing as we started off doing "Boys Don't Cry" which was pop anyway. We just rediscovered it and since then have been able to mix in whatever we want.'

For 'Let's Go To Bed', given Smith's reservations, it was paramount that they produced a video that helped redress that balance – that was what the single was all about, after all. Similarly, Robert was desperate that the video should make it clear that the record was virtually a novelty, a piece of mindless pap that had little to do with the Cure. Smith wanted to look mindless so that no one could accuse him of taking the record seriously.

The Cure had made a number of videos but had failed abjectly to do anything vaguely interesting with the medium, a surprise given the richness of songs such as 'Charlotte Sometimes', which carries the dubious distinction of having probably the worst video ever. Robert grasped this shortcoming and its future importance, saying, 'I wanted to do something with dumb humour,' and went through a few video showreels and eventually asked to see whoever had made 'Bedsitter' for Soft Cell. Enter Tim Pope, who had only just begun to work as a video director, having started out by working for a company that helped politicians polish up their public image. 'In the evening, I nicked all the equipment and went out filming groups like the Psychedelic Furs who were playing pubs at the time. I got my stuff together and showed it people and then met up with Stevo who was Soft Cell's manager and a bit of a nutter in those days and we took it from there. Then I met Robert and he told me they were really disillusioned with it all at that point and they'd just go along and see how quickly they could make them and who could look the bleakest as a joke – they weren't really that doomy, they just wanted to look like that.'

Once Tim Pope joined the fray, Robert began to grasp the possibilities of video – for the first time, a Cure video actually employed colour rather than being shot through some grey mist. Robert was pleased with the results, noting, 'It achieved its aim which was to make me and Lol look completely stupid, a surrogate Tears for Fears video. We were trying to shatter the illusions about us being sullen and remote and living in darkness.' The video was shot with the lights on and featured a Robert Smith that the public had never seen before, an eccentric, oddly endearing little chap who seemed faintly bemused by his surroundings, squirming under the spotlight while Lol performed an idiot dance in the background that resembled someone having a seizure. Already, Lol was the video scapegoat, Robert painting his back and then allowing him to fall through a collapsing bunk bed. The Cure were using make-up in a garish, amusing manner rather than the threatening horrow-show from *Pornography* and the whole piece was a great success. The Cure had finally found a video director with whom they could work and this was fundamental to the way in which their future was to pan out over the next decade.

Nineteen eighty-three remains possibly the strangest, most turbulent and hectic year of Smith's career. During those twelve months, he toured with two different bands, made records with three different groups and released his biggest hit single to date, 'The Lovecats'. It was ushered in by a Banshees tour of the Far East and Australasia but on his return, while Siouxsie and Budgie went off to record the Creatures' first album, Robert and Steve Severin finally found the time to make a record together, and work began on it in March as Robert's record out of the Fiction contract. Already, though, he had taken on board yet another new project having been approached by Nicholas Dixon of the Royal Ballet with a view to providing some music for him to work with – ultimately the project was shelved after an unsuccessful trial run on BBC's *Riverside* arts programme.

Throughout March, Smith and Severin embarked upon a backbreaking schedule that was to produce their album, *Blue Sunshine*, so named in honour of a B-movie concerning a batch of industrial-strength LSD that turned its users into bald homicidal maniacs exactly a decade after taking it. That gave a pretty good indication of the subject matter of the record which is perhaps the most amusing one that Robert has ever been involved with. Surprisingly free from self-indulgence, the album revolved around grotesque but blackly humorous stories such as this. As much as any other enterprise of the time, *Blue Sunshine* successfully altered perceptions of Robert Smith and the Cure. The pairing took the pseudonym the Glove, from the murdering mitten in *Yellow Submarine*, appropriate since the album was ridden with blue meanies who were chased away by some of the sunniest psychedelia heard this side of 1967.

For the duration of recording at Pink Floyd's Britannia Row studios – a sly joke in itself – Smith stayed at Severin's London flat. Convenient it may have been but comfortable it wasn't. 'It was a real attack on the senses when we were doing it. We were virtually coming out of the studio at six in the morning, coming back [to the flat] and watching all these really mental films, then going to sleep and having really demented dreams and then as soon as we woke up at four in the afternoon we'd go straight back into the studio so it was a bit like a mental assault course in the end,' Smith remembered later. Severin explained his hopes for the record as 'having more of a specific personality than say the Banshees or the Cure . . . something a bit softer, more introverted . . . an idea of what me and Robert are like as people, our relationship, but it's basically an album and that's where it's gonna stop'. Robert declined to sing all but a couple of songs on the record and so Jeanette Landray, Budgie's girlfriend, was drafted in to fill the breach. She later confessed to having no input into the record whatsoever and it is her oddly detached persona that somehow moulds the whole thing together. She comes over as a spaced-out narrator of a madman's fantasies.

Fantasy was the central theme of Smith's work around this point, since he was often drawing quite heavily on his dreams to provide himself with lyrical ideas, reflecting, 'I've always thought it was a shame not to use your dreams because you spend so much time asleep and you're always dreaming, so I've taught myself to remember them and relive them, purely for entertainment, though sometimes I use them as inspiration.' The Glove's record perfectly illustrated that internal feeding frenzy as the splatter movies he gorged on during the day seeped into the dream sequence lyrics he wrote in collaboration with Severin.

Parry's fears for the future of the Cure appeared to be justified as Smith found himself so heavily enmeshed within the Banshees' camp and so thoroughly disenchanted with everything that surrounded the

Cure. He and Parry were still at loggerheads. Parry had made it clear that he didn't want Robert to sing on the Glove's record since he feared over-exposure although he was understandably concerned as to the consequences of the project's success in terms of its impact on the future of the Cure. There were already overtures from Polydor too – they were keen to amalgamate these two 'difficult' acts into one alternative super-group. Insiders at Polydor suggest that they had given up hope of the Cure ever making any kind of breakthrough, their hopes resting on Siouxsie. If the two could merge into one unit, Polydor logic insisted that would be the final push the Banshees required to enter the big league. If that thinking ever had any validity, and it's hard to contemplate anyone with such a pathological aversion towards making concessions as Robert Smith playing second fiddle to Sioux for any length of time, it was finally and irrefutably dashed in April 1983 when the Cure were offered a rather late promotional slot for 'Let's Go To Bed' on BBC's *ORS* show from Manchester.

Quickly assembling a group that included Brilliant's Andy Anderson on drums and Derek Thompson from SPK on bass, Robert chose instead to play 'One Hundred Years' and 'The Figurehead', 'to everyone's horror' as he recalled, presumably to remind those who had forgotten that the Cure weren't just about 'Let's Go To Bed'. 'I actually enjoyed it, which I hadn't done for two years,' Smith explained, though it's obvious that he was beginning to experience withdrawal symptoms from his band. When the *ORS* offer came through to the Fiction offices, 'I said yes, even though there wasn't a group, just to force me to do something . . . after a year, I wanted to sing again so I started up the Cure again.' It was all the impetus that he needed and he was quickly ensconced within the studio once more with a follow up to 'Let's Go To Bed'. This time, his aim was a more serious dance track, featuring electronics and a similar sound to that which had so pleased him on 'One Hundred Years'.

Looking to work within a more structured and disciplined environment, Smith recruited Steve Nye as producer following his work with the Cure's Hansa contemporaries, Japan. Confident of its potential, Smith was vindicated when 'The Walk' became the first Top Twenty hit for the Cure on its release in July 1983, though it caught plenty of flak for its similarities to New Order's seminal 'Blue Monday', released a couple of weeks earlier. They toyed with suppressing the single but finally agreed to go ahead, leading New

Order's Peter Hook to suggest that while he didn't mind people being influenced by his group, 'The Cure have been taking the piss at times.' In fact, many of the similarities were simply the result of the technology of the time which offered a relatively small range of programmable sounds when compared with those available today – on its release, the Glove's *Blue Sunshine* had many of the same sounds on it and work had begun on that in March.

Again Tim Pope was recruited to produce a video for the track and such was the disorientating wash of colour that he came up with, it was rejected by *Top of the Pops*, and the group had to turn up at the studio again. The first time Robert had Porl in tow, and Phil Thornalley returning for the second appearance. 'The Walk' represented a move forward for the visual partnership, Robert and Lol both contributing by changing clothes and make-up for each take and generally hamming it up. Lol kept the same dance steps that he had used previously while Robert took the opportunity of developing his character which was becoming strangely feline, a little cloying and faintly ludicrous given his previous track record. By now, the Cure were attracting a new audience and old fans were having to reassess their relationship with a band that were no longer the Bergmanesque harbingers of doom that they'd taken them for.

The *ORS* show along with this new interest in videos had had the required invigorating effect on Robert and in August he assembled a new Cure to play Cornwall's Elephant Fayre, preparatory to a brief tour of America, *Pornography* not having taken them that far. In keeping with Smith's insistence that he tour with people he knew and could get along with, the vacant places were filled by Andy Anderson, who had acquitted himself so well on *ORS*, and Phil Thornalley. Somehow within that punishing schedule, they found time to check into Studio Des Dames in Paris to record the third single of Robert's fantasy trilogy, 'The Lovecats', as good a single as they had released and one which cemented Robert's place in the garden of Great British pop eccentrics at a table next to Syd Barrett, overlooked by Genesis-era Peter Gabriel busily dusting down a lawn-mower. The sessions are fondly recalled by all concerned, Lol remembering it as 'an old record company studio, like Abbey Road, with instruments lying around. All the instruments on that session were acoustic, the opposite to what we'd done on "The Walk".'

'The Lovecats', once it had been doctored by engineer Dave Allen, seemed to be musically modelled on Disney's *The Aristocats* with its mutilated scat jazz feel but it was the first song to ask questions about Robert's new interest in visuals, although he continued to complain that 'doing the videos is the worst part of being in a group'. He did admit to Pope's influence, acknowledging that 'we had no interest in videos at all until we met Tim'. The song was an ideal vehicle for Smith and Pope to work on and its imagery strongly hints at a writer looking beyond the simple confines of the recording studio. The video was a raging success, again taking the squirming Smith a little further forward, a little further away from the Smith that had written and lived *Faith* towards a more user-friendly incarnation that could do exactly what he wanted to in any style, any time; the ideal situation for the creative artist. Witty, inventive, raucous and technicolourful, 'The Lovecats' finally broke the old Cure mould in every conceivable way, freeing Robert totally, *Melody Maker* gushingly terming it a 'masterpiece of disorientation'. Except . . . he wasn't happy with the great success the singles had won. 'Having too much success just stifles you. After "The Lovecats", everyone wanted us to reinforce this new status, so we savagely underpromoted everything. That way we could still make the records how and when we want.'

The greatest worry on the horizon was that although he was organizing a different Cure and breaking out of the stereotyped situation, Smith was falling into some of the traps that had led him into such decline a year earlier, most notably the astonishing amount of work he continued to take on. Losing sight of the volume of his commitments amidst their incredible variety, Smith may never have fully grasped just what he was letting himself in for, but there was no time for any breaks throughout 1983 and well into the following year. Robert was determined never again to allow the Cure to become the be-all and end-all of his existence as it had effectively been from 1978 through to 1982, but he was still allowing music to absolutely rule his life. Having not fully recovered from the rigours of *Pornography*, Smith was simply storing up trouble for himself, though given his masochistic outlook of the time, that was probably the attraction.

More indicative of his fluctuating opinions, however, was his decision to play live once more as the Cure. While he clearly felt the desire to go back on stage and sing, it was apparent that he could only do so by playing the old songs since there were few new ones available. To do so would nullify part of the work that had been done to distance the Cure from that past, a fact Smith conceded following the Cornish show, worrying that by recognizing their history, they had compromised the next step forward: 'I didn't want to do those songs ever again,' he complained. Having bravely destroyed the Cure's long-standing reputation by kicking it to death with the singles, it was a capricious move to return to the old material.

There was little time to fret, however, for as soon as the Cure were back home, the Banshees were off to Italy to play some shows and make a video of their first single to feature Robert, a cover of the Beatles' 'Dear Prudence', a psychedelic legacy of Severin's and Smith's fascination with all things Fab. From there, the Banshees prepared for two shows at London's Royal Albert Hall at the end of September, concerts which were filmed and recorded for release as the double LP and concert video *Nocturne*. By this stage, Robert was beginning to flag under the strain of playing McGeoch's guitar parts and expressed concern about his own imminent collapse, though he declined to do anything about it as intermittent recording continued through the rest of the year on the new Banshees record. By now, though, Robert had accumulated sufficient ideas to make his own record and so in September work began on *The Top*, leaving Smith in the terribly schizophrenic situation of working virtually as a session player one day and running the entire show the next.

Having seen 1983 as a year to shy away from responsibility, the year was set to go out with tensions running high as Siouxsie and the Banshees began to tire of Smith's peripatetic activities, understandably miffed at his failure to concentrate absolutely on their record, while he in turn grew tired of their assumption that the Banshees were the only group in the world that mattered: 'I'm just there, I'm just the guitarist with the Banshees. They get a bit fed up with me doing other things. My attitude towards the Banshees is more fragmented than theirs – I beat them at pool, they get ratty.' Polydor's attentions intensified too in the wake of 'Dear Prudence' 's impressive top three chart placing, so Smith found himself as besieged as he had been when the Cure were going through their most hectic phase, though, in the course of a Banshees interview, he played down the importance of the single, saying, ' "Dear Prudence" is not trying to open another door so we can eventually ingratiate ourselves a little bit more into the popular consciousness.'

His only escape was that which had served him well through his life; after the Elephant Fayre show, Robert said, 'We don't make records unless we have a wealth of experience to write about. It's got to feel worthwhile. At the moment we're storing them up to do another . . . the idea of the Cure stopped with *Pornography* and won't be carried on again until we do another album and I sit down and seriously do something.' Having spent months hanging around as a Banshee while Sioux and Severin did the publicity chores, he had a sheaf of lyrics and songs ready to go. Robert Smith was ready to escape back into the Cure.

Chapter Ten

CHRISTMAS 1983 saw the release of *Japanese Whispers*, a compilation tidying up the three singles and their attendant B-sides – the Cure were back and more popular than ever, a perplexing, but gratifying experience for Smith, Tolhurst and Parry. Robert said: 'Now the Cure could go away and do anything – I can experiment within the Cure now.' By employing Smith's often undervalued but uncanny ability to produce memorable pop melodies, they had conspired to reshape the Cure, but the videos had proved to be every bit as important in this transition.

Prior to Tim Pope's involvement, all people had to take away from the Cure were memories of claustrophobic, nasty, sometimes aggressive, sometimes maudlin songs with no discernible personality on which to hang them. Robert came to see the mistake that he had made and set about correcting it with the help of Pope, building this entirely new character behind whom he could hide but with whom he could experience some sort of release, simultaneously giving the wider audience a personality to attach to the music. In today's climate, ear-catching music alone is rarely enough to make an impact; people want stars, or at the very least personalities. Robert Smith would go on to become the ideal pop star, a throwback to an earlier generation, but that complete transformation was as yet still some little way off. Intelligently, he had been using the Banshees as a guide for when that day came: 'I saw with them how that kind of hysteria is generated around a group and so when I was at the eye of the storm it was easier to detach myself from that.'

Robert had begun tentative recording of what was to become *The Top* in September 1983 but real work commenced in December and January 1984. Not surprisingly, the Banshees, who were concurrently working on their new studio record, *Hyena*, were less than enthralled and tensions began to run high between the two camps with Severin acting as something of a mediator. He could understand that Smith was torn in two directions but remained exasperated: 'We always knew he'd be taking December and maybe January off to record *The Top* but we started recording as long ago as June so at the start it seemed such a long way off it wasn't really important. We had to start speeding up towards the end and even then it meant we had to mix the album without Robert which is a pity because he's really good in studios and it's always useful to have another pair of ears.' Siouxsie was rather less tactful, however, saying, 'Fatboy Smith has nothing to do with the album except that he played on it.'

She took a particular dislike to Robert's lack of total concentration on the matter in hand as well as his lack of punctuality – often he would arrive at the studio only to see the others pointedly leaving, requiring him to do his guitar work alone, with just Mike Hedges, the erstwhile Cure producer, as company, something to which he didn't respond well, and which increased his dissatisfaction. 'When we were doing *The Top* I was still very discontented with everything and I thought recording with the Banshees would help me regain my enthusiasm but it had the opposite effect and after a while it got to me . . . it wasn't really me in the Banshees because I was so tired most of the time I was functioning on remote control. It allowed me to go mad for a time. With the Banshees I had no responsibilities, I just had to turn up and play guitar. Badly. Just used to turn the effects pedal full on which is your basic Banshees sound.' This was a later admission for, at the time, he had tried to appear a full-time member of the group, telling *Melody Maker*, 'There's a set of criteria we set in the Banshees which aren't verbalized, they're just there . . . nothing's done without a reason behind it.'

In all fairness to the Banshees, Robert did have other things on his mind, being required to play virtually everything on *The Top* as Phil Thornalley was away in Australia fulfilling prior commitments with Duran Duran. This gave him the opportunity to play bass, an instrument he enjoyed, but which made for difficulties in the studio since everything had to be pieced together instrument by instrument rather than by the more conventional means of at least structuring a backing track with a band playing together. This is at least partly to blame for the lack of coherence on the album since the finished songs were never really identified until they had actually been completed by this piecemeal process. Robert received some help from Dave

Allen who co-produced it with him and Chris Parry, after his sterling work on 'The Lovecats' remix.

Determined to keep up his kamikaze timetable, January also saw Robert recording with Tim Pope. '"I Want To Be A Tree" was a real laugh, a real piss-take,' admits Pope. 'In America at one point, they were calling them "Tim Pope Videos" and I felt really strongly that they were not Tim Pope videos, they were Cure videos or Siouxsie videos or whatever. So I recorded this song which I wrote when I was fifteen, this really stupid song and I did this video to go on my showreel. I asked all the people I worked with like Robert and Siouxsie to come along to slag me off on the showreel, and I really liked the idea of me stepping into their shoes, a real piss-take of what was going on in America. The *Whistle Test* people saw it and asked to show it and I was very iffy about it but it went out and I couldn't believe it, because it was supposed to be the most stupid, crappy thing ever and within a week I had five offers of record deals which was a sign of the times! The Cure said they'd record it with me so we went into the studio and Robert played everything, totally fucked it up, made it sound like shit, the video went out, I played a support gig to the Psychedelic Furs at Hammersmith Odeon with a ten-piece group, no rehearsal, did four songs, it turned into a fucking riot and then I retired. That was the end of my pop career, but my annual royalties pay for a curry so what else do you want?'

Pope was clearly joining Smith's exclusive coterie of tried and trusted friends with whom he's happy to work, but the two have maintained a personal distance, easy enough considering the Cure only do a couple of videos a year which means they don't have to spend too much time together. However, it's a conscious decision by both parties, as Pope explains. 'I don't know him that well – I know him really, really well in a way because we've got the longest relationship between a director and a group, but I very rarely socialize with him, I always go to the parties and stuff but I don't really know the bloke. So a lot of the stuff is my preconceptions and ideas of him.'

With recording largely complete, the Banshees embarked on a brief UK tour having released the 'Swimming Horses' single which sported a video that captured Smith in a highly unlikely white shirt that appeared to have a clothes hanger still in it. By now Robert was beginning to be regarded as something of a joker, the light relief within the Banshees, illustrating just how far and fast things had moved within two years. The strain was starting to tell for at the end of the month he complained that he hadn't had a day off throughout the entire year – his diplomatic faculties, never abundantly obvious, had also deserted him, as he spent his time comparing the Banshees' single unfavourably with the latest Cure release, 'The Caterpillar'.

This was the fourth record to feature a Pope video and several recurrent in-jokes were making themselves felt – Robert's extensive range of two facial expressions, his finger dancing and immobility, his obvious lack of comfort with his body and the lumbering awkwardness that Pope exaggerated, and the incredible colour that they employed. Oddest of all, Smith was now gaining something of a teenybopper following as these videos translated a wriggling, sulky little boy lost and embarrassed by the attention into a kind of teddy bear, his expanding girth making the comparison fairly accurate. Can it be any coincidence that as the partnership has progressed Smith is shown as having huge paw-like hands and bears an increasing resemblance to the Honey Monster in the Sugar Puffs adverts which Pope also directs? *The Top* was an antidote to that slightly saccharin if still disturbing portrayal, as it was to be the most terrifying album the Cure had released, completely unexpected in the light of the singles.

It was not so much the subject matter that was frightening but the fact that it was clear that its creator was on the edge of a cliff screaming his head off without having the faintest idea what he was screaming about. Smith recalls *The Top* as 'an anomaly, it just sticks out on its own, I don't know what was going on. It's fucking deranged' and on its release in May 1984, virtually everyone agreed with his diagnosis. *Melody Maker*'s Steve Sutherland noted that 'the more I think about it, the more I reckon either Smith's gone mad or we have', though Danny Kelly suggested that, 'even the flagship band of the cleansing turmoil of the late seventies can sink into truisms that smack of self-indulgence . . . the Cure is as painful as the disease'. As with any record that Smith is involved in, it had its moments of pure delight such as 'The Caterpillar' but at other times it appeared to be coming from the void. 'My stuff always comes from a lack of faith,' he'd said, but for the first time it sounded as though he lacked faith in himself.

Smith had clearly not resolved any of the personal traumas that had assailed him during the first phase of the Cure but here those dramas were couched in such bizarre terms that the only course of action was to fear for the singer's sanity, especially following even a cursory listen to his vocals on songs like 'Dressing Up', 'Piggy In The Mirror' and 'Bananafishbones'.

Life wasn't made any easier by the studio's location, Martin Rushent's Genetic in Reading. While recording, the Cure personnel stayed in a local pub with the inevitable results, Lol recalling that the drinking barely stopped throughout the process. Robert agreed, saying, 'It all happened between 1982 and 1984, I think I just went totally mental but I was young enough to recover from it. I was totally obnoxious not because we were famous but because we'd earned enough money for me to buy enough substances to abuse myself. I took an extraordinary amount of drugs around that time.' Parry was worried for Smith's health and remembers, 'The album was a struggle. Robert looked terrible, puffy faced, eyes bleary, sores on his lips. He was always listless. I was worried that he was going to have a heart attack and I told him after we'd finished, driving back home in the car, "You know, there are a finite number of records we can make this way."' Smith must have been ill indeed to allow any artistic control to be surrendered to Parry.

Yet Smith's eventual recovery began within those frenetic sessions, although Dave Allen described Robert's attitude at the time as terrifyingly obsessive. By a process of osmosis, Porl Thompson began to edge his way back into the group. Still working as Parched Art with Undy Vella, he spent some time at the recordings as was usual, just to get a feel for the musical direction and, while there, he was asked to play saxophone on the album. Having already done a couple of *Top of the Pops* and other TV appearances with the Cure, he and Robert found that they were able to get on well together, to the point at which he was asked to go on tour with the Cure in April. Thompson was a multi-instrumentalist, and his ability on guitar and keyboards fitted the bill perfectly since Robert alone couldn't provide all the guitar parts and Lol likewise regarding the keyboards, on which he was still very much a novice. Importantly, though it was presumably a simple piece of self-delusion to protect him from further punishment, Robert refused to admit to the existence of a permanent Cure at present, confessing, 'I feel responsible for everything that happens to the Cure and at the moment that's just me.'

The songs on *The Top* swung across the whole gamut of Cure emotions. 'Shake Dog Shake', the opener, and 'Give Me It' were hangovers from *Pornography*; savage slabs of fiercely aggressive loathing. 'The Top' had the same resonance as anything from *Faith*;

'Dressing Up' was introspectively melodic; 'The Caterpillar' was swooning, summery pop of the sort which the Cure were now coming close to patenting; and 'Bananafishbones' simply a wriggling oddity that gave Robert the chance to express the impishly distrait personality of the bloke who was appearing as lead singer in the Cure videos. 'The Empty World' indicated that he felt it was Simon's pride that had lead to the collapse of their relationship, his misinterpretation of what the Cure were about fuelled by his delight at being in a band, yet it suggested that the door wasn't permanently closed to him.

Although the work on *The Top* had seen Smith in a thoroughly exhausted state – and the music reflected both his listlessness and confusion – he appeared to be reconstructing the future of the Cure in his own mind. With himself and Lol as the mainstays of the band, having Porl back on board was, for someone who is so emotionally attached to the past, a comforting and reliable presence. It's a recurring paradox that Smith almost treats the Cure and what it represents in terms of its personnel – a like-minded gathering of good friends – as a security blanket and yet everything about the Cure's music and structure is the very antithesis of security. It is that friction which has powered much of their output. Over their first four studio albums, Smith's role as auteur had become increasingly apparent, squeezing out anyone else's input. However, his creative partnership with Tim Pope was beginning to suggest to him that there were other ways of operating and that collaboration and co-operation might, after all, boast hidden attractions. Pope's arrival on the Cure scene was absolutely pivotal in that here was someone who could actually be treated as a creative equal, a novel experience for Robert who had hitherto always considered himself pre-eminent. After *The Top* he was to concede: 'I need other people around. On *The Top* there was just Lol and Andy and I played everything except drums and it was just the worst record we've ever made. There was no input or criticism of anything.'

Their way of working together was individualistic to say the least but it heightened Smith's appreciation that others might be able to contribute to his vision. Pope's version of their partnership is vivid, if simple. 'We meet up, he'll say something, I'll say something back, we pretend we understand each other, which we don't, we talk a couple more times on the phone, then basically meet up on the day and have a laugh. Actually, not a laugh, they sit around and watch TV while I slog away setting up shots, they then come out and do their bit. But he's great to direct.' The idea of someone actually directing Robert Smith is one which takes some getting used to, but right from the off such has been the success of their work together it has helped change Smith's perception of those around him. By the close of recording on *The Top*, Smith was looking ahead to the idea of returning to the group format again, but this time encouraging a level of input from the others even if the buck would still ultimately stop with him.

His experiences with Siouxsie also pushed him away from what he termed his 'fascist phase'. If his desire to relinquish responsibility had initially led to him joining the Banshees, he quickly grew tired of his diminished status within the group and therefore found himself experiencing the ignominies that Dempsey, Hartley and Gallup had gone through. Having considered himself to be domineering, he found that the Banshees 'was much worse! I found out I was a really benevolent character after meeting Sioux! . . . I'm glad I did it but I'm glad I'm in the Cure not the Banshees.' Certainly internal relations deteriorated quickly over the *Hyena* sessions and, while in Europe with the Cure in May, Robert decided that it was simply impossible for him to continue as a functioning member of the Banshees, for the very sound reason that he was spreading himself too thinly and driving himself to the edge of a breakdown. He said, 'I tried to keep it going for a few months but it just got too much for me. I was just falling over all the time.' Unable to speak to the group personally, he left a long message on Severin's answering machine, eventually cancelling a couple of Cure shows at Severin's behest to fly back and talk things through. However, following a torturous flight, Smith felt so ill that he went straight to his doctor who told him that he had to stop work immediately. Smith refused but used this advice as clinching proof of his need to quit the Banshees. 'I've never felt so bad in all my life as when I was with the Banshees . . . I just reached a point of total collapse,' he said later.

Their reaction was understandably angry, Siouxsie in particular being upset that Smith hadn't been 'brave enough' to tell her face to face, going on to complain that his 'desire to be a pop star ground everybody down to one of the lowest points the band's ever had . . . he claimed that "Dazzle" was ruined by the strings but he wasn't involved in *Hyena* and his comments on it are wounded pride. He was welcome to contribute but he didn't so that's his tough shit. It wasn't an ideal arrangement and we both sort of fell out. There were a few scenes where I kicked him in the goolies. He used to come strolling in three hours late and I hate that kind of drippy, lazy approach and he used to shuffle around which irritated me a lot.'

Robert countered in 1992 with: 'I think she's bitter that I left. To Siouxsie in particular, they are the most important band in the world. I felt stifled by the Banshees; they had very set ideas about what they should be doing and I just wanted to be involved in a more varied musical world. I think that she wanted to subjugate me to her will and it never really worked. I think that I was the first male that she'd come across that told her to fuck off, basically. Everyone fawns over her twenty-four hours a day.' For all the personal bile that came out later, Robert's departure was the inevitable consequence of eighteen months of quite ridiculously intensive work, work which was used as an escape from the mental strain of *Pornography*.

Mental states continued to fascinate Smith and he began to discuss the end of his own career, saying, 'I just don't want to have bits of me falling off in public . . . I like living in my own reality but I can't perpetuate this otherwise I know I'll become really rubbish, so the point where I stop working in contemporary music becomes increasingly close. In fact it's very close.' Smith had simply resolved one crisis by opting for another, but now the time had come to start again with a clean slate. He gave up smoking saying that he didn't want to be dependent on anything but revealed that he had had a drink every night for a year. Once again he complained that 'people want someone like me to exist, to put things on my shoulders like that I'm an alcoholic or something'. He did accept that his position had its dangers though telling *NME*, 'I'm really stable but a lot of it is through mental discipline . . . we're in a very Kafkaesque situation where you have to control your urges.' This had obviously been difficult over the preceding two years. Paradoxically, he also noted: 'That's part of the make-up of someone who's in the group. You don't stop doing something just because you know it's going to do you harm. That would be very boring.'

A brief break in the summer gave him the chance to sift through his cassette collection in order to compile the *Curiosity* selection for the tape version of *Concert*, the live album which was due in October. *Concert* was very much a reaction to the opulence of the Banshees' *Nocturne*, Smith consciously steering clear of criticism of this project by ensuring that the Cure's record was little more than a superior bootleg, a hard-sounding, dirty record that did actually feel like a concert recording rather than something concocted in a studio with overdubbed applause. The album also served as some kind of reaction to the excessive publicity that the video-friendly Cure were getting in the pop press, an attempt to redress the balance since live performance has always been the real yardstick with which to measure the band, their best concerts far outstripping their recorded work. Over the same summer, he finally bought a flat in London, tiring of staying with other people during his regular jaunts to the capital to deal with assorted record company businesses. He and Mary moved into Maida Vale in August.

The respite was a short-lived one, for the Cure set about a three-month trek around the world in September, during the course of which they succeeded in dropping another member, this time drummer Andy Anderson who had been feeling the effects of the Cure way of life, eventually going on the rampage in a Japanese hotel, causing Robert to sack him, the first time he had done so face to face. Landing in America, Phil Thornalley contacted Vince Ely who had previously played with the Psychedelic Furs but who was now working as a session player and doing advertising work. Ely was only available for eleven shows and so it was left to Thornalley to fill the breach again. Although they had toyed with the idea of using Lol as the drummer again, they rejected the proposition and in November recruited Boris Bransby-Williams from the Thompson Twins: 'I knew Phil from when he'd engineered the Thompson Twins' stuff and he suggested I do it so I joined up halfway through the American tour.' Williams fitted into the band immediately in one of those happy accidents that brings together like-minded individuals. The set gradually grew in length as he came to terms with their songs, having bought all their albums on getting the job. It was clear to Robert that Boris would be a great asset to the band since his sense of humour and general outlook was sympathetic to his own, he enjoyed the Cure's music and lifestyle and soon indulged in the by now endemic sport of Lol-baiting. These were the ideal credentials for a member of Team Cure and Robert set about a campaign to persuade Boris to forsake the Thompson Twins and the infinitely better wages to join up with the Cure – given the current fortunes of the two acts, Boris clearly made a very wise decision.

The final piece in this particular jigsaw came with the resignation of Phil Thornalley who had organized his own recording contract and was busy himself making demos for his debut album. Thornalley initially left the Cure in February 1985 only to decide shortly afterwards that he might actually like to stay with the band instead. Lol suggested, 'When his solo stuff wasn't going so well, he wanted to come back but by then we'd moved on. I think he wished he hadn't burnt his bridges.' By that time, Robert and Simon had buried the hatchet and were working together on some new demos. Lol told *Record Collector* in 1993, 'We did some demos and Simon came along and then he was back in. There's been many versions of the Cure but Simon was always one big part of it. So it was better to have Simon because he's the Cure's bass player.' It was an attitude that Robert shared wholeheartedly, one explaining Thornalley's introduction to the group, a role which was entirely temporary as far as Robert was concerned: 'He was just in the group as an experience and there was never any question he was going to stay in the group.'

As 'The Empty World' had hinted, Robert seemed to feel that Simon would be back in the band at some stage. Simon was then in a group with Matthieu Hartley, originally called Cry but soon trading as Fools Dance, a throwback to Robert's own label Dance Fools Dance, which he had coincidentally reactivated for a single by Animation that quickly sank without trace. Simon's membership of another band might have proved an obstacle for others, but by now for Robert it was just an irrelevant detail, after all: 'I'd been in the Banshees for eighteen months, we'd made *The Top* and I felt really unhappy with what I was doing, then I got back in touch with Simon and suddenly we had a group again and that's what saved me. I was really happy when we did *The Head On The Door* [the next album] and the year that followed was brilliant. It was like starting all over again. If I hadn't had that I wouldn't be sitting here now. I think I would either be hospitalized or . . . I'd be eating banana butties somewhere.'

Chapter Eleven

OR TWO years, Robert had been in flight from his responsibilities, his role as provider for Fiction Records and assorted Cures being too much for him to bear, as perhaps was the knowledge that he had forced his closest friend out of the group simply because he himself was too set on a personal course that allowed no time for others. Those two years had been long, intermittently painful and often beyond recall as he attempted to push himself to the limits almost as if driven by some kind of death wish, perhaps fuelled by some remorse over his less than ideal treatment of Mary and over his selfishness in general.

One of the cornerstones of his mental and physical decline was his alarming appetite for recreational pharmaceuticals. Those around him such as Chris Parry had warned him of the potential consequences of his behaviour but Smith, quite naturally, paid scant attention to them. However, with his interest in the music rekindled, he came to see that in order to be sufficiently fit to go and make more records within a group whose set-up he was finally happy with, things had to change. 'I just realized one night that I couldn't go on as I had or I'd end up a complete half-wit. The funny thing is, when I stopped so did the band. It was like since I didn't ask for it to be around, nobody else bothered. As a result, the whole character of the band changed.'

Smith's attitude towards drugs had not changed particularly and he certainly wasn't going to run a 'Just Say No' campaign, since he still felt that hallucinogenic drugs were perfectly all right, but he simply concluded that he had pushed his mind and body quite far enough for the time being and so drugs were barred from recording sessions.

For those sessions for *The Head On The Door*, it was imperative to Robert that Simon be on board as a full-time member of the group.

Recalling the problems with the Magspies and not wishing to recruit anyone in addition to Simon, Smith tried to gradually ease him back into the band. He was not present for all of the demo sessions and it wasn't until recording was about to begin in earnest that Robert finally asked him to join the group again, by which time his colleagues in Fools Dance had a pretty good idea of what was coming.

Those recordings got under way at Angel Studios in London in March 1985 and, if other drugs were not available, the better financial position of the group allowed them to buy in alcohol virtually by the van load, something which didn't exactly speed up the process of making the record, although it did help create a good atmosphere, enabling the group to get to know one another in an enjoyable environment. After all, Simon and Boris hadn't met while Porl and Simon had only occasionally seen one another over the previous few years. While the others seemed either better able to hold their drink or were able to rein back at the right times, Lol was generally sent home night after night in a taxi, unable to continue working, the start of the deterioration in relations between him and Robert.

Another reason for the lengthy recording process was the attitude of experimentation that they employed, with Smith keen to use a different drum sound on each track, a move clearly suggested by the presence of Boris who was by far the best drummer the Cure had ever had, technically excellent but also a truly inspirational interpretive player. Lol agreed, saying 'The Cure were a band made up of friends and it wasn't really how good you were at what you did, it was whether you had the same ideas. But with *The Head On the Door* we were much more accomplished because Boris was there.' It was Boris who provided the musical foundation which finally made the Cure sound like a band rather than a collection of individuals for the first time. The challenge that this provided Smith as a songwriter and as producer in tandem with Dave Allen was met with a diverse range of styles that allowed the group to show sides of their character that had never been apparent before.

After the paranoiac density of *The Top*, the clarity and simplicity of *The Head On The Door* was a breath of fresh air, achieved by the very fact that the Cure were now very much a band who could play together in any environment. That they were playing in such a way meant that there was far more space left within the music where previously Robert had been filling in all the gaps. As a result, the music they were making, even the more intensely personal tracks, was immediately rendered more accessible without resorting to crude compromise in the way that Robert had with 'Let's Go To Bed'. Once the record was complete, there was little question that it was set to become the most commercially successful Cure record to date.

Its success was heralded by the release of 'Inbetween Days' as a single in July, which peaked at No. 15. This was the first hit single for the Cure that simply came together from the normal recording sessions rather than being constructed purely for the singles market as the *Japanese Whispers* songs had been. 'Inbetween Days' set off a mass of signals in its wake about the Cure's new attitude, musical stance, approach and status as a group and *The Head On The Door* became their most eagerly awaited album to date. It represents the furthest extent to which Robert plays the commercial pop game nowadays, as he admitted in 1987: 'The media is very reluctant to play certain types of music. It's so formatted that you have to get inside and something that conforms so that people are made aware of who you are and then you can start to gradually slip outside again and they'll still play your records which is what's happening. We do think about singles, I always try to write one single on purpose.'

More than just the one; *The Head On The Door* was filled with potential single releases, to the extent that it almost became a compilation record in the mould of *Three Imaginary Boys*. The variations in style and approach were held together by a far more relaxed attitude within the group – Smith described it as being stupidly childlike. The enjoyment they had derived from making the record was transparent, something of a first for the Cure. Naturally there were songs that had echoes of previous albums – 'Push' for instance was about irrational hatred and called to mind *Pornography* – but even these were infectious.

Clearly Robert's disposition was affected by the people around him and by now he was close to assembling a team that would endure – Dave Allen continues to produce their records, Simon is still in the group while Porl and Boris have only very recently handed in their notices, so Robert must have been beginning to think that he had been successful in creating this 'alternative' version of reality for himself. As early as 1985, he was saying, 'I've never felt this comfortable with a line-up, now it's more a group mentality than just me because everybody's involved in it, for the first time since me, Simon and Lol.' That degree of stability impacted upon the record.

The interesting question is just how did he manage to come upon his collection having had so much trouble in the past?

Importantly, he and Porl had had few problems in the Easy Cure days and after Porl had left, they then had the chance to get to know one another again in a working environment when Parched Art were doing the band's sleeves. In his capacity as artist, by regularly attending Cure sessions, Porl had the chance to learn at first hand just how Robert liked to work and therefore how best to work with him. By the time he was formally a Cure again, he knew precisely what would be expected of him and how to make it work, saying that 'it's really just a group of friends that play and enjoy each other's company', exactly the spirit Robert was trying to create this time around.

Simon was simply glad to be back in the fold and had three years of working in the Cure to look back on and learn from. Like Porl, he was careful not to step on Robert's toes in the first instance while, in his period away from the band, he had made a conscious decision to avoid being argumentative wherever possible having had further run-ins with Matthieu in Fools Dance and not enjoying the experience of fighting seemingly all the time. For *The Head On The Door*, Simon was once again Robert's closest friend and concentrated more on rebuilding that relationship than trying to find areas of difference between them. Robert's reputation as a stern taskmaster had gone before him in an exaggerated fashion via the press and so Boris would have been well aware of what he might have been letting himself in for – to find that Robert was actually human after all and that recording sessions were actually enjoyable made his life easier as did the fact that his sense of humour ran along the same lines as the others'.

Much of the change had of course to come from Robert himself, for it was his attitude and approach that would determine who remained as a functioning member of the band. He was still in charge of the group as the songwriting credits on *The Head On The Door* proved. He justified his actions with: 'You have to have some kind of discipline and that only really comes from one person having control, not in a dictatorial sense but because the idea of a committee dilutes things. If we were all to have exactly the same say we'd just argue but I would never have a group that had people in it that didn't want to be in it. You can't have security within a group like the Cure.' Practical reasons had also contributed since 'it was a very structural record and I had to sacrifice any inspiration that could have come out of the five-piece for the sake of getting the record done because there were so many other things to be done after it'. It's also likely that Smith would not hand over the reins he guarded so jealousy without studying his associates closely over a period of time, such as during a tour. Clearly he had recaptured some of the naive enthusiasm he had originally had for making music and being in a group, an enthusiasm that had been gradually ground down by the problems of the previous few years. His decision to free himself of extracurricular activity and instead concentrate solely on the Cure paid dividends in that he wasn't the physical wreck that he had been, giving himself enough time to prepare and record while the absence of drugs meant that he was able to focus more closely on what the group were doing and that none of them were suffering/enjoying the after-effects of anything other than alcohol. That being the case, everybody was pulling in the same direction until the session closed for the day or they were rendered incapable.

Having benefited from Tim Pope's input on four videos prior to these sessions, Smith was getting to grips with the idea of collaboration and in consequence he was also making a greater effort than before to accommodate his colleagues, not in terms of the writing as yet, for that was still very much in his hands, but in giving them the opportunity to express themselves within the framework of the songs or to criticize aspects of the material they were working on. Having seen Siouxsie and the Banshees make what he felt to be a poor record in *Hyena*, a project on which he had little say, he better understood that if the Cure was to be a group, he needed to encourage the others to contribute even if ultimately he chose not to act on their ideas. At its root, Smith missed the camaraderie of the group and concluded that if he was to be able to enjoy that again, he would have to allow contributions from all quarters.

Having survived the self-imposed trials of the previous couple of years, he also made a very real effort to change his way of thinking, saying, 'I used to be very morbid but you get to the point where you either accept it and make a career out of it and metaphorically kill yourself or you dismiss it and use it to create an environment in an absurd and slightly deranged way which is what I chose . . . the songs are a way out because whereas I would have done something really stupid, now I try and understand why I feel like that because I realize that the less I feel like it, the more I'll enjoy myself.' From time to time, Smith would continue to draw on his darker emotions but he had now formulated a way of dealing with them away from the Cure such that they took up 10 per cent rather than 50 or 75 per cent of his waking moments.

Having built three very powerful records from his preoccupation with death and his atheism and the conclusions that spring from that, Smith now seemed to be mature enough not to let them dominate his life. By the time the Cure came to make *The Head On The Door*, it was clear that, having weathered the recent storms, there were now no obstacles left in the way of the band and that the Cure could go on for just as long as they chose, while financially Smith knew that there was no longer the remotest chance that he might be sucked back into that ordinary world. His future in material terms was secure – if there was still no faith in any life beyond this, he might as well enjoy this one and take advantage of all the possibilities that were opening up to him as a consequence of his success. He admitted, 'I'm much more able to cope with the things that used to destroy me.'

The dread name of Morrissey comes up often in Smith's conversation not least because he still smarts at the idea that anyone should call a band the Smiths as a description of anonymity. However, Morrissey's morbid wailing and humourless diatribes on his perpetually miserable state must have struck Smith as particularly ludicrous, things worsening once writers began to compare the two lyricists. Smith said: 'To be commended as a top lyricist in the same breath as Morrissey would be a sort of condemnation. If someone said Morrissey's a really great lyricist and you're not far behind, I'd probably hit him.' That Morrissey should be selling records by the truckload and yet still portraying himself as an abject failure whose every waking hour is filled with anguish is patently ridiculous at a time of mass unemployment, homelessness and rampant poverty. Smith had no intentions of becoming such a laughable caricature of himself and therefore elected to enjoy what he had, giving himself scope to sometimes dip back into that mix of emotions when the mood was too strong to overcome.

Presentation was of course a central part of that escape for Robert Smith was regarded as a witty pop singer courtesy of the group's video output and now, if he came up with a darker song, people tended to assume that it was just a one-off rather than the mainstay of his creative output. 'Inbetween Days' continued this trend with its fast-paced video which romped through the song in a pastiche of the Beatles *A Hard Day's Night*. Featuring a camera first attached to Porl's guitar and then swinging from a wire, it caught the summery mood of the song, though Robert was nearly decapitated for his pains when the camera was originally weighted wrongly and swung within inches of his head. 'Inbetween Days' has become a central video in the Cure canon, one which helped crystallize this new feeling of unity within the group, built on the jokes and ideas of the previous films and brought in new themes such as the Day-glo socks that were used to comical effect – since then, there has been a sock strategically placed in almost every Cure video. Tim Pope recalls that 'We wanted all this blurry colour over it so we put a bunch of my old socks underneath this very complicated camera rostrum but when it came back and I saw it I thought, "Jesus Christ, they actually look like socks, they don't look anything like blurry colour."' A likely story . . .

Probably Pope's greatest contribution to the world of the Cure was in being probably the first person not to take Robert seriously and to attempt to make him look as foolish as possible: 'I believe people who watch videos want to see people suffer so I make them suffer as much as possible,' Pope says, Smith adding, 'He always throws something in that he knows I'm going to loathe.' Although it's done in an affectionate, mocking style it has helped prick any pretension or pomposity that might have lurked in the Smith psyche. Tim creates an enjoyable environment, saying, 'We have jokes with each other, every time he goes on TV he slags me off, Mary christened me "Pap" but then again when I get the chance I usually call him a fat bastard so I suppose that's fair enough!' In fact, between them they have constructed a Robert Smith who is every bit as much an alter ego as Ziggy Stardust was to Bowie in the early seventies, Smith having the considerable advantage of not having to give himself another name, thereby neatly avoiding the need to appear a complete idiot.

This construction began right from the off with 'Let's Go To Bed' and Robert's discovery of the ancient art of finger dancing. 'I moved him into shot,' recalls Pope, 'and he was just standing about looking a bit of a dork, a bit shy, so I had to find him something to do with his hands and we just got carried away with it from there. That's the joke, really, we just make the same video over and over again, the same things happen, the same things turn up, nothing different ever happens. The number of times we've had fucking socks in a video . . .' Cure psychology was changing rapidly with Robert happier than for some time and Pope's work attempted to reflect that for with 'Inbetween Days' there was a real sense of fun. 'Every shot I do always has some relationship to the psychology of the Cure,' avers Pope. 'Robert and Simon are really good mates, they always hang around together and they look the same so I use them as mirrors whereas Lol's always been the scapegoat. When I got the rushes back for "Close To Me", there were close-ups of all the others lying in that wardrobe at the end with the odd shoe coming in or something but when I got to Lol's close-ups there were fists coming in, they were holding him under the water, so it became really heavy going! He had a very important role in the Cure around then.' Robert described Lol's appearances as Stan Laurel-like.

The creation of Smith's filmic character that sometimes approached cartoon-like proportions caused him to walk a fine line – throughout their career, the Cure have been keen to show themselves as they really are, Smith in particular refusing to put on an act to mask his own shyness and reserve but allowing people to see him for what he is. However, he had become used to the idea that to take the Cure further and to increase the fanbase, image had to take its part. In building their image, Robert has generally chosen to take just one facet of his personality, that part of him which finds making records absurd, is bemused by the entire publicity machine and finds the very idea of making videos stupid, from which has come this delirious character who plays on the fringes of the pop world. While the videos show the audience a piece of the Cure and especially of Robert Smith it is far from being the whole thing – early videos showed the Cure as the music suggested they would be, hard faced, cold and unrelenting, but by now they had come to accept that that sort of brooding intensity simply does not translate to the world of promotional film. The Cure on video are wholly separate from the Cure on stage or record and it's a Cure that is in one regard totally unimportant and yet has provided the way in for many fans who have then gone on to discover and become fascinated by the core of the group's work. As Smith suggests, 'We have hits mostly to change our audience. I hate the idea of the same faces year after year.'

Robert has used the scope that video has given him to write different kinds of songs – the visual imagery has become increasingly colourful, as in songs like 'Lullaby', while the witty video treatments have allowed him to continue exploring heavier emotional themes without him being categorized as a misery. As a performer, too, his success on video appears to have offered a release that has had commensurate benefits on the live stage. Smith has admitted to grave doubts about his appearances on video since he feels inhibited by the contrived nature of the whole experience, yet these videos have been one of the group's great success stories. Gaining confidence from that Robert has become increasingly impressive on stage, using tools such as his distinctive silhouette to elicit crowd response, knowing that his immobility and discomforted, squirming embarrassment have been legitimized by the videos they've done. By now, the Cure had become a truly visual group with Smith as its focal point. His smudged lipstick, spidery coiffeur, enormous trainers and baggy jumpers spawned a thousand imitations within his audience, Smith confessing that some looked more like him than he did! The video character has been in some measure extended to the stage, giving Smith someone to project his feelings onto. That he plays to the gallery is beyond doubt for as Chris Parry has noted, 'Like any good artist, he lives within other people's perceptions of him.' Strangely for someone who was so desperate to give notice of everything that he was going through, the public face of Robert Smith now bears less relation to the real Robert Smith than it used to. He admits: 'The performance thing is driving me away – I enjoy it less because it's less and less like I am when I'm away from the stage.'

The music, however, continues to reveal what Robert Smith is thinking and this was the case on *The Head On The Door*, Smith having plenty of material to choose from. As a mental discipline he had gone through a period of writing every night until he was satisfied with a piece. 'Six Different Ways' was a song about his treatment of others; 'The Blood' was allegedly about a brief encounter with a Portuguese wine that was alternatively available as a paint stripper; both 'Screw' and 'A Night Like This', the latter dating back to 1976, seemed remorseful; 'Close To Me' a claustrophobic rant against wasted 'days when you just wish you hadn't woken up because it's been such a trial', while 'Sinking' harked back to *Faith*. The most uncharacteristic song was 'The Baby Screams' which let Robert laugh at himself, a throwing the toys out of the pram exercise. This was a healthy new departure for Smith who continued the trend with 'The Exploding Boy', the B-side to 'Inbetween Days', the title based on his appetite for excess.

For the first time, the Cure sanctioned the release of a second single from the album, because, 'As "Inbetween Days" didn't get in the Top Ten, I had a verbal agreement that they could release "Close To Me" if I could do something different to it.' Robert was given the chance to remix 'Close To Me' and Tim Pope obliged with the video clip which went on to become an MTV staple. The irony is that as Robert recalls, 'At the time of *The Head On The Door* we were told by Polydor that we mustn't use Tim Pope. In fact we were told that we wouldn't get any money towards the videos if we used him so we didn't get any money for "Inbetween Days" – that was how strong the feeling was that he was actually holding us back!' Pope was understandably more forthright: 'The formulas are bollocks, I never listen to that stuff which meant at times I was very unpopular with MTV which is a really bad thing in my job! But I've been around long enough to see this happen, MTV suddenly realizes that they've gone up this avenue and look to someone like me to get them out of it, so I become popular – I'm like God with MTV at the moment.'

In fact, Smith remixed the track again for the video, taking off all the reverb which 'made it really dry and even more claustrophobic' as Pope noted. Again this calls up the on-going relationship between the videos and the records for there have often been changes made to the song for Pope's benefit. 'The music has always been fairly visual,' Pope concedes, 'but sometimes when I hear songs I do get a sneaking suspicion about it, or he'll send stuff over and say, "You'll like this one," so maybe there is some influence. The remix for "Close To Me" completely changed the song. Later on, he played me the rough mix of "Lullaby" and I said we'd do certain things with the film and in doing that he actually put the lower voice on the song.'

One of Pope's greatest reservations is that in portraying only one aspect of the Cure, he has reduced their impact: 'I do think video is quite a dangerous and bad thing. There's an argument that it's been bad for their image that they almost misrepresent them because no way does it capture the power they have live because there's no way you can do that on the TV. That's why I try to do it differently and catch a side of them that you wouldn't perhaps see otherwise . . . the point isn't to flatter or to sell the product necessarily.' By the following summer, Pope was given an opportunity to redress that balance.

Chapter Twelve

WITH *The Head On The Door* installed as their most successful album to date, the band went off on the obligatory tour of the world, and in Britain they played some large venues such as Wembley Arena and the NEC in Birmingham. One smaller show took place in November, a benefit in aid of Mencap, confirming Robert's dedication to their cause. He said, 'I've grown to care a lot more about a lot of things . . . I don't worry about dropping out of the public eye, I would just like to become involved in something that has more substance but will still satisfy me. I would like to go into an area of mental health . . . sort of becoming involved in a physical way, maybe making it an issue. Probably the only thing you can do if you're in a group is to bring out something that's otherwise very unnewsworthy.' Smith later pointed out the dangers of advocating social change, saying, 'If I tried to go crusading for things I wouldn't be able to go shopping any more because people would be laughing so much. It'd be awful.' The Cure continued to support Mencap – when *Entreat* eventually came out in 1991 for instance all royalties went to assorted charities of which they were one. 'It's no big deal but the fact that you earn lots of money means that you can do things with it.'

The tour went well with the band atmosphere surviving largely intact yet one gruesome incident came to characterize the American view of the Cure when, at the final show in Los Angeles, just before the band went on, a member of the audience attempted suicide by stabbing himself repeatedly until security guards stopped him. Tragic in itself, it also reinforced the contention that they were all angst and no fun, turning interest in them into a pat shorthand for TV and film writers to indicate mixed-up children – the Steve Martin film

Parenthood uses a bedroom poster of Robert to underline the point that 'this adolescent is confused and miserable', for instance.

The tour aside, Robert had plenty of other things to occupy his time. With the release of *The Head On The Door*, the Cure's licensing contract with Polydor under which they distributed their records had come to its conclusion. Aware that if they left, the label would come up with a spoiling greatest hits package to coincide with their next album proper, Robert circumvented the problem by compiling it himself along with an accompanying video collection 'because I'd rather do it with some control'. *Standing On A Beach*, a line from the debut single 'Killing An Arab', was an undeniably impressive collection when released showing that the Cure had gone through some pretty strange developments over their career but that their saving grace had always been Robert's ear for a good melody line. The change in the group's attitude over time was apparent though Robert made it very clear that this change did not involve the making of any concessions: 'I'd rather be successful and not compromise, but given the choice, I'd rather not compromise.' With the release of *Standing On A Beach* he maintained this attitude, refusing to allow any single release until he was granted the chance to remix 'Boys Don't Cry' and re-record the vocal, a necessary move since his voice had dropped considerably since the original had been made. This time it was a hit, reaching No. 22.

The video collection, *Staring at the Sea*, also did well, but its compilation allowed Tim Pope to further discomfit Robert. '"Charlotte Sometimes" has become a big standing joke between us. When we put *Staring at the Sea* together, whenever he went out of the room, I always managed to have "Charlotte Sometimes" on when he got back. It drove him mad.' Commendably, Robert didn't spare himself any embarrassment, putting all of the Cure's videos onto the compilation. They also worked together on a new video for 'Boys Don't Cry', which featured three young boys miming while a film of the Cure was projected onto a screen behind them, as Pope recalled. 'Robert had the idea of using the kids and then left it to me to find them. I came up with the idea of the shadows with the group playing because I thought it would be rubbish if they weren't in it at all. We got Michael Dempsey back – brilliant, the original line-up – and shot the backdrop with Robert, Lol playing drums which he'd been sacked from, and Michael and gave it [to] the kids. We worked with them and rehearsed it, made them stand like the Cure used to, dressed them how Robert used to dress – still does. On the day I front-projected it so the image was behind them and it was amazing. I got the rushes back and this kid had learned every move, the gestures, the finger dancing, the chord changes, everything. That was great fun.' It was also confirmation of Smith's arrival as pop icon that he had so many definable attributes that he could be impersonated so easily.

Plans were being laid for a return to the studio in September 1986, the group having demoed around twenty songs under the working title *1,000,000 Virgins*. Prior to that, Robert wanted the group to play live so that they wouldn't be going into the studio cold, but would simply follow on from the concert dates which he felt would lead to a better record. Since 1986 seemed to be a year in which they were wrapping up a phase of the Cure with the compilation record and video, they decided that a concert film was the obvious accompaniment particularly as they would be playing many of the songs for the last time. It was also vitally important that people should be reminded that first and foremost the Cure were a group, central to which was their reputation as one of the strongest live acts around. For Robert, 'Playing live was one of the motivations in being in a group. It adds a dimension to the group and enhances what you do in the studio. There's a physicality with concerts that you can't get with records . . . live is much more what the Cure is about than the videos.'

There were arguments put forward by the record company for numerous directors who they felt were better equipped to take charge of the project, but naturally the Cure wanted to use Tim Pope and, as usual, the Cure got their way. It would have been sheer folly to use anyone else given the closeness and success of their relationship hitherto, though given the cost of making feature films, it's unsurprising that other counsel tried to prevail. That it didn't was all the better for the film since it was unlike any other concert film you could see. The setting was an enormous ampitheatre in Provence that Pope found and which dwarfed the spectacle of U2's 'Red Rocks' show, the obvious comparison being Pink Floyd's Pompeii film. This, though, was purely live footage and for better or worse it had the atmosphere of a live Cure set designed to appeal solely to Cure fans, thus eliminating any chance of a cross-over audience – a stupid concept anyway. For some tastes *The Cure In Orange* seemed slowly paced for cinema release, rigidly following the group's set list as it did, a set structured for an audience that was actually participating in the concert but as a piece of Cure history it remains powerful viewing. There are stand-out performances all over the place – 'Faith' is absolutely compelling, vividly illustrating Robert's depth of feeling for the song and its subject matter while it also shows his trust in the new line-up as he had not played it since 1982. 'Close To Me' is hilarious, Robert attempting to dance then collapsing with embarrassment halfway through; 'Give Me It' is suitably frenzied; 'One Hundred Years' aggressive and the list goes on. A couple of ponderous songs loosen the atmosphere but these serve to bring out the best in the songs that surround them.

Pope was able to bring the band to life on the screen – especially at its cinema release where the size of the spectacle was brought home more fully to the viewer. He employed several of the tricks he'd been using in their promotional videos, shooting 'Close To Me' in close-up to reproduce the claustrophobic feel, 'Inbetween Days' benefited from the swirling camera work while again he was keen to point out the interplay between the members of the group. Yet he had approached the film with a degree of trepidation. 'Robert asked me to do it and said, "We don't want a real film-maker to do it, so you'll have to," so I agreed! I went off to see them and sat at the front of the stage blocking out the audience to see what they looked like and I thought, "Fucking hell! They don't do anything!" Literally, they just stand there. Robert stands there, moans a bit and sweats like a pig and that's all there is! Then I watched a bit closer and there are all these subtle eye movements and stuff – Robert looks at Simon, he looks back and it obviously means something. Essentially they're a really boring band but in fact they're one of the best live bands you could see, so I tried to get that epic quality. I was really chuffed because Robert said, "Thanks, that's the first time I've seen The Cure live." It's an interesting film because I tried to build it with that psychology and totally alienate any non-Cure fans that might see it. They play for real, there's no posing, it's very straightforward which is what I wanted to film.' Robert was in agreement, saying, 'The film was just to capture what we were doing – we only had the one night to get it right. It was supposed to be a Cure film about the Cure . . . I wanted to catch us at that point because we were playing really well. It makes me feel like I do on stage, it makes me squirm about.'

One problem which Pope couldn't overcome was Robert's change of image. Oddly for a retrospective type of film, he cut off his hair which had become one of the Cure trademarks. Tim responded, 'He's a bastard! He did that just to spite me because I'd based the whole thing around them being hairy little bastards, which is what most of the videos are based on. I always say they're like a group of hamsters, but he went and shaved his fucking hair off just before the gig and he came out grinning just to wind me up. That's why I put the wig thing in, the idea of Simon yanking it off Robert's head and throwing it away leaving Robert with the crew cut. I didn't have any say in it, he did it just to fuck me up – he's such a conniving bastard, he'll do what he wants when he wants and no one can control him.'

Smith without his bouffant was strangely interesting, for his use of make-up was accentuated, allowing the audience to reassess just how much he has embraced the idea of theatricality and used it as a channel for his emotions to come through, though he is still patently ill at ease on stage, hopelessly cumbersome, often hiding behind his hands and muttering unintelligibly to the crowd between songs. It's an odd paradox in that he so obviously enjoys the idea of playing live and can so often get lost within the songs and yet, at the same time, another side of him is desperate to get off the stage to the safety of the dressing room. The shorn locks also made him appear much more aggressive, lending an extra edge to songs like 'One Hundred Years' and 'Push', an edge that was often smoothed over and softened when Smith appeared physically softer – without the hair, he looked more like a bank robber than a pop star. Smith was right to describe it as 'the most aggressive thing you'll see at a cinema this year' and it made a suitable finale to *The Head On The Door*. The group took a brief break in Toulon where they were apparently besieged in their hotel before returning to the studio in France where they were to record, having agreed to sign once more with Polydor despite offers from Virgin Records. Interestingly, Polydor's contract is with Smith alone, not the Cure.

Recording started in Draguignan, but quickly moved on to Miraval studios, a residential studio way out in the countryside, far removed from the distractions of the city – 'very secluded and isolated' was how Robert described it. 'We thought it would make a nice change, though it's more like an asylum than a studio at the moment.' Although the site itself was idyllic and attractive enough to seduce any group into recording there, there was an ulterior motive to the decision not to record in England this time – the tax man cometh.

The year 1986/87 was their tax year out of the country to save on the Inland Revenue bills, an interesting concept for Robert who so regularly professes not to be bothered about money. On the other hand, he probably felt he could make better use of this money than Thatcher's government, and who's going to blame him for that? The consequence of this decision was that further mixing had to be undertaken at Compass Point in Nassau – where brass was added to 'Icing Sugar' by Andrew Brennen who, as legend has it, Robert saw playing in a terrible bar-band – and at ICP in Brussels, while concert rehearsals were carried out in Dublin.

The *1,000,000 Virgins* sessions, soon to be renamed *Kiss Me Kiss Me Kiss Me* so that Robert could put an enormous close-up of his mouth on the album cover, were a radical departure from recent Cure projects in that this time each member of the band wanted to be involved and their ambitions were encouraged by Robert. Preparatory demo sessions had taken place in North London prior to them leaving the country, and once recording began, they found that there were around forty songs at their disposal which immediately pointed the way towards a double album. Robert was responsible for the bulk but the others chipped in too. 'I sometimes get very angry at them because they don't do enough but it's now worked itself into a stage where everyone feels obliged to contribute because they know how bitter I'm going to get if they don't.'

Robert's plan to get the group playing together as a band paid immediate dividends, for they quickly picked up from where they'd left off, rehearsing and running through a song for a couple of hours and then recording the basic backing track live as a group, moving at a steady pace without any undue pressure and recording one or sometimes two tracks per day. 'I wasn't in any desperate hurry to get it finished,' Robert admitted, 'because the process of making it is just as much fun as anything else. The *Kiss Me Kiss Me Kiss Me* stuff was one of the best periods of the Cure, it was good fun . . . it was the first time we've been a group since *Pornography* when we could just sit down and play and I'd look at Lol or Simon and know what they meant.' Having whittled the original bunch of songs down to a core of those that really inspired them, they finally recorded twenty-six songs for Robert then to work on.

Much of this amply illustrated Robert's new more relaxed style both as a person and as the leader of the group. He was far more open to suggestion and just as willing to try things out and see what happened – if nothing came of them, then that was fine too but at least an attempt had been made and nothing had been lost in the effort. Similarly, Robert allowed greater spontaneity into the sessions – with almost every other Cure album in the past, a very definite mood or subject was firmly decided upon well in advance and the music was shaped to fit in with those ideas. With *Kiss Me Kiss Me Kiss Me* there was no fixed concept prior to recording and so the songs were allowed to grow and develop, each member throwing in new ideas as they rehearsed them.

Miraval itself had much to do with the level of enjoyment that the band got from the sessions. In the south of France at the tail end of the summer they had pleasant weather, a degree of isolation, the opportunity to take girlfriends to the studio while they were working, and that inevitably fed into the music, particularly on drowsy, drunken reels such as 'Catch' or 'The Perfect Girl'. The idea of living at the studio per se made the greatest difference, though. Where previously the group had had to work fixed hours in studios in and around London, checking in and out when time was booked, this time they could use the studio at will and were able to live within its environs so that, should the fancy take them, they could go straight into the studio and work.

With everyone permanently on call too, by virtue of their proximity to one another, it meant that everyone had to be ready and willing to put in as much effort as the others, there was little opportunity to skip any sessions and so the unity of the band was further reinforced. They were able to create their own atmosphere free of any other concerns, centred their lives wholly around the making of the record, and that level of concentration conspired to create a coherent whole. Robert was also given greater opportunity to observe the abilities of the others at close quarters and thus came to appreciate them more and consequently was more able to trust their songwriting talents. 'We can get totally involved in it,' according to Simon. 'You're just conscious of it all the while, even when you're not working on it. It's practical and you can build up your own atmosphere.'

The album eventually stretched to eighteen songs and was a more extreme version of *The Head On The Door* in that each song received a different treatment, and a remarkable diversity was achieved. The band also cannibalized their own back catalogue to round up the history of the Cure with songs that drew on their greater experience as writers and musicians. Almost every song could be placed in the context of a previous record: 'The Kiss' and 'Shiver And Shake' were songs straight from the mood of *Pornography*; 'Why Can't I Be You' and 'Just Like Heaven' were sublime pop of a *Three Imaginary Boys* vintage; 'How Beautiful You Are' had the feel of *The Head On The Door*, and 'A Thousand Hours' expressed the futility with which *Faith* had concerned itself, the same lack of any kind of belief which had made so many of Smith's songs harrowing listening.

The sessions were of course as much a social junket as work and, given Miraval's location amid French vineyards, a little social drinking took place, early reports suggesting that the group and entourage had demolished 150 bottles of wine within a week. While the French declared a national holiday on the back of these soaring profits, the Cure did still manage to manufacture some internal trouble. Allegedly, Lol was drinking far more heavily than the others and, as had apparently happened with the previous record, he was often unable to play. By this stage things were very clearly reaching crisis point between the two founders of the band. Again, Smith alleges that for 'Shiver And Shake' – which has to rank with the most vicious, spiteful rants that Smith had ever committed to vinyl, far more aggressive, even in intent, than anything from *Pornography* – he forced Tolhurst to stand in front of him while he sang, a savage piece of vocal butchery that had gone through nineteen previously unsuccessful takes: 'The lyrics show, I think, quite clearly, my disappointment and anger at [Lol's] deterioration both as a member of the group and as a human being,' Smith later said. It was done in just one long rant, but apparently he'd had an early version of the song almost a year before, suggesting that dissatisfaction with Lol had been running high for no little time.

Lol, on the other hand, recalls that Miraval was 'a good thing, to lock yourself away from the big cities and get your head down. That way it becomes a much more personal document . . . we knew what we did best, we felt a lot more comfortable as a band. After *Pornography* I think *Kiss Me Kiss Me Kiss Me* is my favourite album.' Just prior to the *Kiss Me* sessions, Robert had been saying that while Lol's keyboard skills left a lot to be desired, he couldn't envisage the Cure without him. With two such conflicting stories, it's hard to piece together exactly what did go on, but it was obvious that Lol's position as scapegoat was reaching disturbing proportions as the video to the album's first single, 'Why Can't I Be You?', indicated. Smith's explanation was that, 'We wanted to be Five Star and that's what we thought they were like. We were very self-conscious about the dancing so we thought we ought to dress up. We put Lol in the Humpty Dumpty with a strobe light strapped to him and he went completely berserk.' Is he an epileptic? 'He is now.'

The persecution went further for according to Pope, 'While he was in there, I had this camera attached to a bit of rope and I kept kicking him underneath and treading on his feet to make him dance and they were all spinning him around. I didn't generally participate in the Lol-baiting because it reached heights I couldn't possibly go in to, but I think that was the ultimate thing I did.' Smith also notes that, 'The obvious phonetic depiction of the word "can't" [Lol as Louis Armstrong peering from between a pair of lips] was nothing to do with me. It's the childish side of Tim Pope's award-winning nature.' Pope also continued to hark back to other videos – the swinging camera of 'Inbetween Days' simulated this time by the band running around the camera to gain a similar, if trashier, effect.

Originally written by Smith as an answer to the question that people often asked him – 'some of the time, I wish I was someone else. When I'm being pointed at I wish I could disappear' – this was by far the most incredible Cure/Pope film to date for it featured the band in all manner of disguises, Robert as a teddy bear, for instance, which Pope must have used as a piss-take of Robert's burgeoning status as a sex-symbol, the adjective 'cuddly' appearing in relation to him with increasing frequency, much to his dismay. Count Boris naturally took a part as a vampire and then maintained the distinguished line of drummers in drag, while Lol was ruthlessly persecuted as usual. Given that this was in a promotional video and was supposed to be funny and entertaining for a wider audience, perhaps the idea of suffering to achieve the desired effect might not be such a problem, but within the studio environment it's a different matter altogether.

Where a gang mentality exists, there's always a scapegoat just as other roles are adopted – leader, confidant, joker, etc. Within a pressurized situation when people are thrown together for extended periods of time for almost twenty-four hours a day, tempers fray and the scapegoat becomes the centre of attention which is fine when the scapegoat is willing or able to fight back. However, once that becomes impossible for whatever reason, the tormenting, as in this case, can reach appalling proportions. At this point, if, as Smith avers, he organized Tolhurst's stay at a health farm and took all reasonable steps to make him understand the nature and severity of his position within the group, failure to respond on Lol's part would only attract contempt from the others.

Given the alcohol-fuelled environment which tends to distort reality and can often fuel aggressive behaviour, Tolhurst may have reached a point at which he could no longer retaliate against wave after wave of criticism and practical joking. He was later to suggest that the attitude of the others had broken down his confidence and given him no chance to reassert his place in the group: 'I became very ill and lost over a stone in weight. It was a vicious circle – I drank for confidence but later I lost my confidence because of the drink, or the constant abuse, and became unable to perform.' If that were the case, no number of health farms could compensate for the lack of self-esteem which would be reinforced every time he found himself in the group's company. From the band's viewpoint, however, while they were working long and hard to ensure that the record was right, it's easy to see that anyone not pulling their full weight while still deriving the financial benefits would be less than popular. The Tolhurst situation is a very complex one, one where the true facts are known only to the participants, information that was to ultimately go before the courts in 1994.

Happily, internal bickering did not reach the depths that the Cure had known before around *Pornography* and, for only the second time in their history, the exact same line-up had succeeded in making a second consecutive record together. It was an album they were justly proud of given its consistency over eighteen sprawling tracks, and it was on that note that they concluded the record with 'Fight', the oddest song they'd recorded, a song about dismissing thoughts of defeat, about carrying on in the face of adversity, sticking to your guns and not surrendering, a far cry from the defeatism of 'Faith'. Musically 'Fight' was something of a new horizon too, almost in the mould of 'Kashmir' from Led Zeppelin's great double album *Physical Graffiti*, and it was this kind of song which bore out the rectitude of Robert's decision to bring in the others as composers for, musically, this one was largely down to Porl, while another, 'Icing Sugar', came from Simon. These were new avenues that the Cure were exploring, songs that Robert would not have written but which became identifiable Cure pieces once the band had worked on them – Robert's desire to use their talents did not, however, stretch to using Porl's country and western ideas.

If the Cure had discovered glasnost, democracy was still a way off. 'We used to try and maintain democracy,' explained Smith, 'but it just led to confusion, the whole thing of deciding by committee was turgid. It's not dictatorial but the final decisions are up to me, there's this unspoken thing where what I want happens. I find it very hard to compromise, I know what I'm looking for and what I want, so if differences arise time after time when we're really doing this for fun, the group changes. If the personalities don't work then people leave. The most important thing is making the records, doing the concerts and the spirit inside the group. It tends towards me taking over because it's not in my nature to delegate so I take responsibility on myself.' Robert, once again, was exposing his reservations about having complete trust in anyone in the same way that he had right at the start of the group.

Gallup, a veteran of those early stabs at democracy, agrees to the extent that 'we just go off in weird directions if someone doesn't have the final say'. As an outsider, Tim Pope has a slightly different view: 'Robert is their spokesman, he always says it's a democracy when it's painfully obvious that it isn't and he just lies through his fucking teeth, he's such a bloody liar, though if the others say no to something, he does listen to them sometimes, particularly with Simon.'

Given the mood of freedom in the camp, Robert was choosing to play around with vocal styles – there were two basic drum treatments that they used when on the previous record they had looked for a different one each time. This time around, Robert looked for a different vocal approach each time. On some, his voice was so cloyingly sweet it sounded as if it might rot his teeth but on 'The Kiss' – the album's opener and outstanding song, driven along by a stunning guitar introduction that had some of Robert's finest-ever playing, all played in one take – he was savage, his voice ripping out of the speakers; then again he might try a kind of jazz feel with 'The Perfect Girl', he might just simply howl as on 'Shiver and Shake' or try a soul vocal for 'Hot Hot Hot!!!' As Robert proudly explained, 'We're still a hand-puppet group, we can be really dumb. U2 and Simple Minds can't be dumb, they're too grandiose and important.'

That last song again drew dividends from the new working set-up since much of it came together at Miraval, Robert teaching Simon the bass line, Boris picking that up and then Porl adding the guitar figure, giving a final result which Robert likened to Chic! In general, Robert's writing style was a little less ambiguous than on earlier albums, though again he fought shy of specifics, not wishing to tie the songs down to single interpretations, while simultaneously protecting the guilty. He drew on French literature again, this time with Baudelaire who provided the inspiration for 'How Beautiful You Are' and its dismissal of the idea of a perfect love, territory that he'd previously covered on *Seventeen Seconds*.

The change in style was beneficial to Smith. Previously, writing lyrics had been problematical, but this time he had twenty-seven lyrics available and simply chose the most appropriate. This wealth of material ensured that the group would be able to produce the double album that the music demanded, and have extra opportunity to experiment and develop ideas leading to what *Melody Maker*'s Chris Roberts called 'a subjective sublime . . . album of the year'. When the time came to take those songs on the road, the Cure were able to play a whole variety of sets depending upon the mood of the group from night to night.

Their tour began in South America in March 1987, under conditions designed to test the *esprit de corps* of the most seasoned band. Among the problems were the internal flights, Simon remembering, 'In Argentina we went on some really dodgy flights with bits of the plane falling off and we came out the other end shaking and dripping in sweat.' Shows were oversold, leading to riots by those ticket holders locked out, the unpopular local constabulary were attacked during the shows with the unwanted side-effect that the band themselves were often struck by flying missiles. Robert once was hit full in the face by a Coke bottle, naturally causing him to stop the show and go berserk. Once they had reached the venues, it was literally impossible for them to stray beyond the dressing rooms given the mass hysteria their presence generated in countries only just getting to grips with live British rock music. 'The concerts were really good though, very frenzied,' according to Smith.

Still, the band that plays together stays together, as the saying goes, and the Cure's attitude to one another was strong enough to withstand even this level of pressure, a pressure that was unrelenting around the world as they – or at least Robert – suddenly became media stars, having reached the point where they now sold sufficient quantities of records to warrant attention beyond just the music press.

This didn't entirely please Robert: 'The fact that we sell a lot of records has everything to do with the fact that they're good but it has a hollow ring because people like Wacko and Michael George sell a lot of records and they're basically shit.'

Lol recalls, 'We did an awful lot of touring. Not only did we play concerts everywhere, which involved three blocks of concerts for six months, we also had to do a lot of promotional work, which we hadn't done before. We did every newspaper, radio station and TV show. After a month it becomes more work than playing a concert every night. Press-wise things tend to change at the last minute so it's more chaotic than a tour.' Given that Robert was the real centre of this media whirl, he stood up to the pressure extremely well, although America continued to prove a trial to him: 'Being in America changes my personality completely. It makes me monstrous, as loud and obnoxious as a lot of the people you meet there.' Generally, though, the atmosphere remained good throughout, testimony to the spirit of the new group. Porl summed it up best, discussing their preparations prior to a show: 'We're a band and we just like to be together.'

Even so, part way through the tour, the Cure recruited a keyboard player, Roger O'Donnell, fresh from a less than enjoyable spell with the Psychedelic Furs. Keyboard player was Lol's role in the group, and the recruitment of O'Donnell does bring into question Lol's contribution at this stage. Robert noted later that he would put coloured stickers on the keyboard to remind Lol which keys to depress, 'But even so, he still made frequent mistakes both in terms of notes and timing.' O'Donnell's talents helped flesh out the group's sound, taking them further away from Robert's ideas on minimalism and helping them produce an enormous, epic sound, suitable for the larger arenas they were now playing, though critics did wonder if the Cure were becoming overblown. At times, this may have been the case, but the effect was rather more dramatic than pompous, achieving the essential scale that stadia demand. The major disadvantage of the big shows was that the band found themselves exaggerating their own behaviour to compensate, Robert worrying that 'some nights I've noticed myself performing, like an animal, becoming the persona that exists in the videos, dispassionate, which my vanity enjoys but which is clearly wrong'. Would there be another Cure tour?

Three further singles came from the album, all enhanced with previously unreleased songs left over from Miraval, along with remixes but, given the multi-format nature of some of the releases, the fans were starting to become a little restless, having become accustomed to only one single from an album and special single-only releases. The Cure audience is, according to a rueful Smith, 'very critical. I think they're young enough to mean it's difficult to trick them. I think it's a piece of piss to sell records to older people because they don't fucking listen. Our audience won't let us get away with anything.' Unlike many audiences who blindly buy anything with the group's name on it, the Cure crowd is a little more sceptical which explains the sometimes disappointing chart performance of Cure singles compared with the albums.

Again Tim Pope had his part to play, the group attempting to stretch the scope of their video performances, the luxury of having to make four films giving them the chance to do different things. While 'Why Can't I Be You?' was wild and wacky, the group poking fun at the video creatures they'd become, 'Catch' was more serious, attempting to evoke the atmosphere of the song and of the summer in France. This was symptomatic of an attempt to show a slightly more serious side of the group within the videos – after all, with the enormous global power of MTV and music programming on TV in general, the videos might be the only opportunity that many fans had to see the Cure and while acting dumb was one part of their nature, it wasn't the be-all and end-all. 'Catch' tried to put the emphasis back on the song and the idea that the Cure could write about beauty as well as the darker side of life, though Robert wasn't wholly satisfied with the results. The video was shot in France using beautiful cinematography in an attempt to capture the idyllic nature of their stay at Miraval. Essentially it was a film of the Cure lounging around in lovely surroundings, though Robert wasn't entirely happy with the outcome. 'It cost twice as much as any other video we've ever made, £120,000. Lol ruined it. We made this beautiful video and this old bastard in coalminer's jeans wanders down the spiral staircase not even bothering to pretend he's playing the violin.'

In the same vein, 'Just Like Heaven' was a cinemascopic mini-film this time with Robert given the chance to act alongside Mary. The film was beautifully shot and lovingly made, ideal for such a gorgeous pop song, Pope admitting, 'With a song like that, it's filled with joy or something, it's just marvellous so people will always think it's a good video, whatever you do.' Robert had even more say than usual on this one because, 'It takes two incidents from real life: the main one happened where it was filmed, on Beachy Head, fifteen years earlier. The song's about hyper-ventilating – kissing and fainting to the floor. Mary dances with me because she was the girl so it had to be her. The idea is that one night like that is worth a thousand hours of drudgery.'

To combat any accusations that the band were becoming needlessly arty, 'Hot Hot Hot!!!' returned to the knockabout format. This time, the Cure were reduced in size, literally, to midgets, Tim Pope suggesting that since Robert was talked of as a sex symbol, this showed him to be only half the sex symbol that people felt he was. This time the Cure appeared to be the six dwarves, Snow White and Bashful otherwise engaged.

The persecution of Lol intensified as the later compilation *Picture Show* proved, the out-takes showing Robert spitting on Lol's head, a connection made not too subtly in the video which looked like a 1960s pop show. The dancing from 'Why Can't I Be You?' was a little more formalized this time, while socks and wardrobes made their by now almost obligatory appearance. The release of 'Hot Hot Hot!!!' completed this phase of Cure activity and offered the opportunity of a well-earned rest. During a break which was to last almost a year Robert and Mary finally got married, on 13 August 1988, with the group in attendance. Robert then surprised himself by getting the Cure back together to make a new record. 'I didn't imagine we'd make another record, that was supposed to be it, the last Cure album looking back on everything we'd done.' Robert was rapidly approaching another milestone birthday, his thirtieth, and given that his twenty-first had started him off on the road to *Pornography*, it was clearly the right time to return to the abyss.

Chapter Thirteen

I T WAS a genuine surprise that the Cure should be recording again given that they had spent almost a year apart and that Robert had stated: 'We'll never announce that we've broken up, it'll just be so long since we've done anything that it'll be obvious.' For a group of their stature, to get the machinery working once again takes a major effort; the record company has to be alerted, crew mobilized, studios booked, the promotional aspect fully organized, tours set up and so, given the financial security that *Kiss Me Kiss Me Kiss Me* had bestowed upon them, the only reason to continue working was out of need or enjoyment. He admitted that 'musically we could come up with ten albums a year, but lyrically it gets harder and harder'. This time around, necessity provided the spur and the group returned after Robert had compiled a set of lyrics that reflected that side of his personality which he had previously given rein to during *Faith* and *Pornography*.

Approaching his thirtieth birthday was a big event for Robert, one to which he looked forward with some trepidation. Given that his songwriting is often coloured either by his lack of faith or his realization that life is fleeting and time is always running out, it was perhaps not surprising that such a temporal milestone would cause him some disturbance, and his new words gave a graphic account of his state of mind. This time, however, Smith's life was a little more stable than half a dozen years earlier, allowing him to cope with the trauma in a less destructive way. Rather than testing himself to the physical and mental limits as he had done, this time he reserved those bleak moments for songwriting and performance: 'The things that bother me seem to crystallize rather than go away. The same things still disturb me but I scream in private rather than in public now. The group is there for me to scream. Each time I do another LP, I wonder whether it's worth releasing it because I could just do it at home and keep it for myself. I have the tapes of the material I was going to do as a solo record but it becomes more and more ridiculous as to why I should go out and do it for other people to listen to.'

Disintegration, as the new album was called, is, according to Smith, 'one of the best, it fits in between *Faith* and *Pornography*'. To go further, *Disintegration* is quite probably the best Cure album and is certainly the definitive one in terms of its exposition of weighty matters, having the considerable advantage over the other two of being less ambiguous and far more accomplished, lyrically and musically. Roger O'Donnell's keyboards provided an epic, almost monumental backdrop that served such mournful subjects well. O'Donnell commented, 'When I joined it was the first time that the band had had an actual dedicated keyboard player . . . now they're an equal part of the group. In fact everything seems to be hinged on the keyboards because it allows Porl to play guitar and Robert to concentrate on singing.' The poignant melodiousness and superb production gave a better realization of what *Faith* should have sounded like, the additional time and budget now available to the group being used to the full. Smith himself has become a far better writer as time has gone on – one of the most selfish of artists, Smith has rarely confused that trait with self-indulgence and has continued to stretch himself as a writer, aware that his obsession with particular subjects means that he has to move on and find new means of expression in order to avoid simply repeating himself.

If age has not granted any greater wisdom, it has provided him with more experience and a wider musical and lyrical vocabulary, an eloquence essential for a writer who wishes to maintain his position of pre-eminence. 'The songs were written [in 1988] when I was feeling completely awful. I was very aware that I was reaching my thirtieth birthday; I realized that I didn't want to go on juggling my different personalities, I didn't want to keep on worrying about the difference between the public me and the private me.' As Tim Pope has it, 'I don't think the video character is like him at all now.'

Smith also said, 'With *Disintegration* I knew I was writing about the things that troubled me for the last time. They're all gone now. It's the last time I'll write about internal disintegration because there's nothing left to say about it now.'

If Smith is preoccupied with the process of getting older, it's a more far-reaching obsession than simply the looming prospect of death, more the comprehension that time is limited and could have been used better. Smith's greatest fear seems to be not death but a life where his sense of wonder is eroded, where everyday cynicism causes him to feel emotions less keenly until he reaches the point of an emotional close-down, the unpalatable evidence of which he can see in so many other people. There's a palpable sense of loss that runs throughout his lyrics on *Disintegration*, not just in the general sense of regret or missed opportunities, but in terms of the hardening of his emotional arteries, a worry that he is losing the capacity to feel as deeply as he once did, a sentiment expressed in 'Closedown', whereas 'Fascination Street' is almost mocking in its dismissal of a futile search for the perfect moment or sensation. It's something that he tries to preserve, though: 'Even when you die, you still don't know anything. I'm not embarrassed to say that I still feel completely at a loss sometimes as to what any of this is about. Perhaps it is more grown up to worry about losing your job than the meaning of life but I wouldn't want to lose that sense of wonder'.

Naturally, the transient nature of any relationship and the depth of his feelings towards Mary trigger off some of Robert's despondence: 'Mary and I were sitting up talking until seven in the morning and we were getting really depressed about what we're going to do and the fact that whatever we do, we're still going to lose each other at some point . . . I feel guilty in the way that I've dragged Mary down to feeling the way she sometimes does because of this side of me that tends towards being very hopeless and dissatisfied with everything and everyone around me and some of that has, I suppose, rubbed off on Mary. But she still manages to achieve far more contentment in a happy way than I do. She still feels genuinely happy and the thing that initially attracted me to her was her ability to be completely abandoned, to be able to laugh in a way that I've never seen anyone laugh before. She's still able to do that and I find I can't, I don't know if I ever could. Sometimes I feel very bitter about it, immensely jealous.'

The trauma Smith attached to the milestone of being thirty was one of the flashpoints which got him writing again. There were other issues which drove him onwards too, most notably the misery of living in London. When a few years earlier he couldn't even bear to be around his closest friends, London must have been unbearable with its seething mass of people. Later, when forced to live there full-time because of recording and business commitments, the sheer horror of having to inhabit a flat surrounded by other people was a debilitating experience. Shortly after their wedding, Robert and Mary decided to move to the South Coast, but in the meantime Robert had built up enough anger at London's brilliant parade to fuel some lyrics. 'Where I'm living determines exactly what I do,' he confessed a couple of years later. 'The fact that I'm not living in London any more has had an enormous effect on me. I don't dislike people as intensely, I'm much more tolerant. Before, I just fucking hated everyone. There are days when I'd wake up and seriously consider the idea of bombing London.'

Along with that, Smith was beginning to feel that their new-found status and their ever-expanding audience were founded on the wrong idea of the band. Having made two records that were pretty diverse in content but which were structured in such a way that there was something for most tastes, Smith was concerned that the listening public had had things far too easy from the Cure and that it was high time their loyalties were tested. He was keen to put something to these new followers that had the same kind of emotional depth and power that their earlier records had had and which was broadly missing from the more recent albums. On *Kiss Me Kiss Me Kiss Me* for instance, once you'd gone past the opening track, 'The Kiss', the rest of it was comparatively easy listening. The time had come to give those new fans who hadn't gone in seach of the back catalogue an introduction to just what else the Cure could do, though he made life easier for them by subtly recycling chunks of old Cure songs – a refrain from 'A Thousand Hours' from *Kiss Me Kiss Me Kiss Me*, for example, found its way into 'Plainsong'. So determined was he to get this new record right, he even took to cutting off his famous hair again: 'I like it short when I'm recording, when it's short I feel ugly and I try extra hard to make something beautiful.'

In such a complex array of reasons for making a record, two others stand out. Given the new level of camaraderie within the group following the delightful experience that *Kiss Me Kiss Me Kiss Me* had been, there was a great deal of sense in seeking escape from this new rush of depressed feelings by playing with the band, channelling the energy into a new record, so that this period could be both documented and turned into something more positive. Equally, having the group around him would help Smith deal with some of these crises. Smith was no longer the same person who had made *Pornography* in that he was less selfish and would no longer inflict punishment on those around him for simply being there, though he said 'I was much more isolated. I'd come in, do the vocal and disappear.' The group's ability to play together simply confirmed the validity of the band in his mind and also let him exorcize some of these demons. Allied to that, *Disintegration* was an exercise to prove to himself that he was still capable of feeling things as sharply as he had ten years before, that he could still create songs of depth and impact from the midst of his own despair. 'I was missing doing something with more depth and emotion and concerts that had the intensity and I wanted to drag the group into doing something that hurt more. I could only get motivated if it was going to be difficult,' he confessed. For Smith this was central because, 'I resent people you grow up admiring who turn out to be the biggest tossers like David Bowie.' Smith did not want to become the 'fucking chameleon of rock'.

Perhaps listening again to *Faith* at the end of the year had a further impact on the direction of the sessions, Robert admitting that 'it disturbed me. I realized that I hadn't resolved anything. I reached the point a long time ago where I don't have any kind of spiritual faith and so I have to find something else, some form of release otherwise everything would become unbearable'. The cathartic nature of *Disintegration* appears to have been that release.

Recording began with the traditional demo sessions which were held at Boris's home in Cornwall at the tail-end of 1988. The band then moved on to a residential studio, inevitably, since they had found that environment so conducive to their work at Miraval. This time the location was a little less exotic, the 48-track Outside Studio in Berkshire with Dave Allen again producing alongside Robert. Allen picked up on Robert's mood. 'For *Disintegration* we were trying to knit it into one long entity so it's obsessively non-diverse.' Again Smith invited material from all the other members in the band, but this time he made it perfectly clear that only certain moods would be acceptable and that the music had to go in a very specific direction. 'I had a key song to motivate me, just a strong instinct to start with, then an idea of what I wanted and went to the group so that we could mutate it. We started with the idea that it would be an hour long, which we've never done before, to allow us to do eight- or nine-minute songs, long strong atmospheric pieces. If you've got a good idea, you should allow it to develop.' When he informed the group of his plans, he had mooted the idea that he make the record as a solo album if they felt they didn't want the Cure to return to earlier stomping grounds, but such was the power of Smith's own contributions and the feeling that the lyrics generated, they were keen to go on. Simon suggested that the idea of using one theme was a good one, Boris recalling that everybody brought songs to the rehearsals and 'the most depressing ones got onto the album'. Robert made it clear that 'it was called *Disintegration*, everyone knew the mood it should have and the musical framework'.

Robert continued the tradition that had been born before the *Kiss Me* album of everyone 'turning up at a pre-album meeting which is five days' drinking before we pluck up the courage to play our tapes, although we do have a rule that says no one should openly laugh. We give the songs points so in that way it's democratic and then we demo those. If there's anything left out that I think we can use, I use my power of veto to include it, but if everyone's not happy with it, it's pointless.'

Recording ground to a halt as soon as the band had gathered at Outside when a fire almost cost Robert his lyrics. 'A heater shorted and it burned everything I own. Because we were here for four months, I'd brought all my worldly goods with me. We saved my lyrics, crawling along the floor with wet towels around our heads. We had to make a chain and hold hands and because I was the only one who knew where they were, I was the last in the chain. We got really told off by the firemen, it was like being back at school. They were saying, "Your life's more important that your words," and I was like, "What do you know?" They were the only thing that was irreplaceable, I thought. The next day, I was sifting through the charred remains and I came upon my wallet and it had two pictures of me and Mary – the first two pictures we ever had taken together – and they were still there although a bit charred around the edges and I was really pleased. I genuinely felt happy about the fire, I didn't feel upset, I felt relief in a very banal way.' Once the band had recovered from the unwanted excitement, the sessions progressed pretty swiftly, although there were distractions, as Dave Allen noticed. 'All the things [Robert] says about liking passionate music are true and you can't be like that twenty-four hours a day, so we end up really only doing something for four or five hours a day and waiting around for the right moment the rest of the time. It's weird, there's a lot of work ethic there and there's a lot of, er, non-work ethic. They do a fair bit of drinking it has to be said.' Smith noted that, 'We were playing through the night which we hadn't done since *Pornography*. Things got very intense, we put songs like 'Disintegration' into a key that I can't sing so it hurt me. It sounds really good from a physical point of view.'

There were a couple of breaks, in the more pop-sounding 'Lullaby' and the sweetly moving 'Lovesong' which Robert had apparently written for Mary as a wedding present. 'Lullaby' was the obvious first single by virtue of its beautifully layered sound and its nursery-rhyme quality, neatly combining that childlike feel with the oft-ignored sinister seam of fairy tales. Robert's nightmare vision of the predatory spiderman cried out for a video treatment, this time Smith producing a storyboard along with Tim Pope that remained fairly faithful to the song. Pope said, 'You can't fuck that up. The basic structure of the idea is in the song even if you could go off in two million different directions.' He also remarked that he felt there was something of Robert's pharmaceutical past hidden within the song, though that was less readily apparent. The mini-movie has gone on to be possibly their most popular video, finally gaining the BPI award as Best Video in February 1990, late recognition of their contribution to the world of the promotional video. Pope maintained reservations even then, saying, 'I just think it's a really terrible medium for music, it's influenced it in a really bad way – a lot of the money that should be going to develop new bands is spent on these fucking useless videos. The thing that I really object to very, very strongly is they pin a song down to a certain set of images and that's something I try and avoid. Sometimes they work and I think a lot of the Cure ones do, because they don't spoil the song, although anyone who ever listens to 'Close To Me' will probably see a wardrobe or feel that claustrophobia, but then that's a reflection of that quality in the song. I see a lot of videos that don't have too many ideas. The director looks out of a window, sees a flagpole and decides to shoot the video from the top of a flagpole even though it's nothing to do with the song. I always throw everything within the song up into the air and let it land in my fetid subconscious and take it from there.'

One of the features of the 'Lullaby' video – other than the obligatory appearance of wardrobes and socks – was its menacing quality, Robert's spiderman being a genuinely disturbing creation. Their *Top of the Pops* appearance was nearly cancelled because his make-up was so extreme, only going ahead on a no close-ups basis in case he frightened the viewers. 'It was a kind of throwaway video,' says Robert. 'Jim Kerr from Simple Minds didn't understand it, my nephews did. Given the choice of audience I'd rather have my nephews. That Simple Minds have been taken seriously for years is quite incredible. Jim Kerr is just a plump Scottish git and he does these awful things like marry Chrissie Hynde. He marries these hideous women and still people like him!'

'Lullaby' featured an endoscopic camera making its way into Robert's mouth, the most extreme version of their fascination with mouths in these films. 'The imagery has been based around orifices and the mouth's been the most socially acceptable one. I do find mouths fascinating and kind of repulsive. They're like a gaping wound in people.'

'Lovesong', the second single, produced a less successful film, the band having got caught up in the power of their live performance, making an abortive attempt to translate that to video. Sitting in an unconvincing cave, Robert, caked in make-up 'to cover his old age' according to Tim, tried to convey the feelings behind the song without any success. Given the level of heart-breaking passion on the record as a whole, live performance made more sense of it than any other medium could and it was a great pity that the Cure didn't choose to make a live film or video from what was titled the 'Prayer Tour'.

'Disintegration', a song that Robert reputedly wrote on his thirtieth birthday – though given the album was in the shops two weeks later it seems a romantic if unlikely story – was a central piece in the album's construction, but Robert marked the melancholy closer 'Untitled' down as being the real crux, with its acceptance of both life's lack of meaning and the need to battle against those feelings. 'That really is the key line in the record, knowing that everything's futile but still fighting, still raging against the dying of the light. I am sometimes overwhelmed by a sense of futility and purposelessness and at that point you have to do something to affirm your existence. I write songs.'

'The Same Deep Water As You' referred once again to Robert's fascination with drowning 'as a part of imagery, just like letting go. It's actually like walking out into the lake sort of drowning, giving yourself. I have less fear of drowning as a death, if you were to reach that point then the sense of giving up would be more perfectly enacted in drowning than any other way of dying.'

'Pictures Of You' was more about holding on and went back to the incident with the fire: 'I realized that I'm clutching old pictures of things, even taken before my birth, to give me a sense that things went on.' Smith has retained the childlike fury that builds on hearing the dread phrase 'before you were born' and his perception of his own existence as the only reality there is continues to fuel the songs, though again the video for the song pricked the potential pomposity by staging a snowball fight in front of some palm trees, filmed cheaply and easily on Super-8.

A rough version of the album was ready for a Christmas playback at RAK Studios where it was being mixed. This party proved to be the catalyst which led to the final parting of the ways between Lol and the Cure. According to Robert, Lol spent the evening getting very drunk and abusive about the record which he felt to be substandard. For Robert, this was the final straw given what he alleged was Tolhurst's absolute non-participation in the recording process. 'He slagged off everything to do with the album, the group and me and just got drunker and drunker. He said the album was shit, because he hadn't played on any of the songs. It was the first time he'd heard them, I think, and he didn't like them – but he was still prepared to take his money and go on tour and suffer it.'

Lol completely rejected these allegations, telling *NME*, 'What had started off as a band where everybody had their influence was getting eroded until it didn't feel like there was anything that you could contribute even if you wanted to. It's funny because on *Disintegration* I actually played on more things than I had for the last couple of albums,' an odd statement given that it was a matter of public record that Robert had written 90 per cent of *Pornography* seven years earlier and actually had less of a say in the writing of *Disintegration*, even if he did impose conditions on the music in general. After a long argument at the playback, Smith waited until Christmas had passed and then wrote to Lol telling him that it was in the best interests of all those concerned that he should leave the group.

Again, the only parties who know what really went on are Smith and Tolhurst and their recollections are almost totally contradictory. If Smith is correct in his assessment of Tolhurst's contribution to the records, suggesting that for the last five years in the band, he was 'dead wood' and that it was his excessive drinking that contributed to that lack of input despite Smith himself making strenuous efforts to help him rehabilitate himself, Smith's exasperation can be readily understood. Given then that *Disintegration* was a record very, very close to Smith's heart in the mould of *Faith* and *Pornography*, Tolhurst's condemnation of the album was not guaranteed to win friends nor influence people.

Even had relations been good before that point, given Robert's regularly stated credo that if you don't agree with me you can find another band, Tolhurst's outburst would surely have ended his tenure. Having been in the band since its inception, he had seen enough people come and go to realize that Smith will only deal with those who share his artistic vision, a hard-headed approach, maybe, but one which has paid dividends, their albums providing the proof. On the other hand, Robert does often appear to be the personnel manager from hell. If his reasoning that Lol should go was acceptable purely on the age-old clichéd grounds of musical differences which the play-back had highlighted, the way he went about it was far from exemplary. If you're going to sack someone who has worked alongside you for over a decade, whatever the provocation and whatever your own feelings, it's surely best to do so face to face – at least that earns a degree of respect from the other party and gives a real opportunity to clear the air and perhaps even conduct matters less acrimoniously. Smith went on record at the time as saying, 'Lol's accepted my reasons for not wanting to play with him in the group any more . . . from 1985 onwards I never had a conversation with Lol because we disagreed about virtually everything. His friends were city beerboys driving about in silver Porsches. The whole social side of his life was anathema to what me and Simon liked. We disagreed about everything. He voted Conservative, he voted for law and order, all the things we used to joke about . . . he just diverged, it's no big deal.'

To say that leaving a band after more than a decade is 'no big deal' suggests that Smith lost his sense of proportion for a while, particularly as he went on to say, 'I've known him since we were six, we're a bit long in the tooth for recriminations.' To justify his actions further, Robert added, 'If he'd come on tour with us in Europe, he wouldn't have come back, that's how bad it is, I was doing that hedonism bit when I was twenty-three and it would be stupid for me to be doing it when I was thirty. The human body's miraculous but it's not that fucking miraculous. It has eluded him that he didn't actually play on *Kiss Me* or *Disintegration* – he wasn't even there. I papered over the cracks and felt a genuine sympathy for him until it reached the point where he was just taking the piss, literally. During *Disintegration* he didn't set foot in the studio. He went there so he was physically in the building, so he could pick up his paycheque. I told him I didn't want him around any more, he'd become a fixture only appearing at meal times and totally out of his head. Lol's never had any musical input and he's the only one of us who hasn't been able to pull back from the excesses of being in the group. When you're a six-piece you've got to have some dedication or it just ends up like a football team.' Robert apparently wanted to see an end to Lol's position as victim, for on the *Kiss Me* tour, 'Lol just drank his way through [it] to such a degree that he didn't bother retaliating. It was like watching some kind of handicapped child being constantly poked with a stick. I said to him before recording that if he didn't assert himself and get involved then there was no way I could carry on seeing everyone using him. It's just become so predictable and detrimental.' O'Donnell backed Robert up: 'He was like a safety valve for all our frustrations which was really sick, by the end it was horrible.'

At times, Robert seems so cocooned within the organization he has built around himself that he loses sight of everyday realities – other people are capable of being hurt too, it's not a phenomenon strictly limited to Smith himself. That he refused to talk directly to Lol suggests either something approaching cowardice, that Smith was too fed up with Tolhurst's behaviour to bother – he did protest that 'it's not my fault if he's got enormous character defects' – or that he simply failed to realize that Tolhurst might actually be taken aback by the news. Whatever the case, Robert might well have saved future aggravation by taking a little time to simply talk things through. This action was not that of a born diplomat, particularly if Lol's accusation that he tried to phone Robert on receipt of the letter, at Robert's invitation, and that Robert then refused to talk to him is true. Lol later put his side of the case, saying, 'It was about halfway through *Disintegration* that things weren't working out too great, I wasn't feeling that well in myself and I guess the Cure psychosis struck again. Big time! I was wondering about continuing when I got the letter, which I didn't think was the best idea, having known someone all that time. But I thought the whole ethos of the Cure had become slightly warped as far as I was concerned . . . it became very undemocratic and a lot of the people around the band, like the record company, found it better that way because they only had to deal with one person. And that was a bit upsetting as over the years I'd put a lot of my life into it. I talked a bit to the others. They must have thought it was for the best because they didn't say otherwise. But I think they'd been put in a position where they had to be seen to be satisfied with the way things were. Otherwise they get to feel uncomfortable, shall we say. That's the kindest way I can put it.' On the other hand, Robert told *Select* magazine in 1991 that Porl had suggested that he wasn't ready to tour if Lol went too, and Simon was even stronger in his opinions.

Tolhurst's inference that the remaining Cures were a bunch of yes-men deserves consideration. After all, Simon, for instance, had taken great pains never to blame Robert for their original split when there were very clearly faults on both sides, while they had all accepted Robert's dominance of the *Disintegration* sessions without any great debate. However, to suggest that collaboration was no longer allowed seems highly contentious when, if anything, it was clear that the group were moving closer towards a measure of democracy. The music they were making made that very obvious for all to hear as Porl's input and that of Simon was plain. Roger O'Donnell also contributed heavily to the texture of the overall sound as well as supplying demos that were worked on in the sessions and became B-sides.

Simon's treatment of Robert is merely typical of any very close friends, who for the sake of their relationship are loyal to one another, at least in public. Tim Pope, though making it clear that Robert was very much the group leader, rejected the suggestion that the group simply accepted Robert's say-so and had seen a movement away from that position as the video progressed. The departure of Porl Thompson in 1993, without any rancour, because there were other avenues for him to pursue, gave further credence to the fact that the band spoke with one voice because they were equally inspired by what they were doing. It seems clear that Robert remained very much the leader of the group as had always been the case, but the *Disintegration* concerts showing that they were very definitely pulling together as a unit. Lol's further accusation that Robert was musically hard on the others while being less concerned about his own performance is refuted by Roger who told *Keyboard*, 'Although we take great pains that everything is played perfectly, Robert actually steers away from musicianship.' Since the Cure and Robert Smith are virtually synonymous and since he jealously guards the reputation of the band, it is unlikely that he would accept sub-standard work from anyone, least of all himself, since he knows how badly it will reflect on him later.

The situation whereby Polydor's contract was with Smith alone is an interesting departure, though given the volatility of the Cure's line up over a period of years, a very sensible one. Smith, by virtue of being the singer and main songwriter of the group, effectively carries the name the Cure with him. While he could not make the records without some assistance, there could be no Cure records without him. The royalty payments that the Cure receive – and Smith has arranged an extremely high rate of 20 per cent which is around twice the normal rate for most artists – are scrupulously shared out to everyone's satisfaction, Smith making certain that all songs are credited to the group nowadays, ensuring that no one loses out financially. If you wish to pursue the line that Smith is an employer of musicians, a line that is less credible now than at any stage in their history, it seems that, at the very least, he is a financially generous employer. One explanation is that the group isn't motivated by financial gain, though this is easy to say when you're in a band that's sold 20 million albums, but it does seem oddly accurate when Smith says, 'If all you're bothered about is the records sounding how you want them to sound and not about being famous and competing for air time, the peripheral things don't matter. People recognize that – we've become more and more successful by default, by avoiding things we've built up a sort of mystique, we've got there through persistence, refusing to go away. I got involved because I wanted to play in a group with other people, I wanted to play music and write songs and I'm not interested in anything else.'

With Lol's presence clearly repugnant to Robert, right or wrong, this was another added element in the chemistry that made *Disintegration* such a potent record. Acting as an irritant, Lol would only have drawn further bile from Robert in the same way that he suggests 'Shiver And Shake' fed on that anger. The other members of the Cure can take pride in the fact that the solidity of the group was not damaged either by this on-going feud, or the brutality of much of the music, ingredients which had almost destroyed previous incarnations of the band. One thing they seemed unable to arrest was Robert's absolute determination never to tour again once *Disintegration* had been hauled around the world. Robert's attitude was: 'I like playing live but I hate touring.' With that in mind, Robert ensured that the tour itinerary in 1989 took in places they hadn't visited before including those countries behind the Iron Curtain that were now opening up to rock music, the Cure, now a five-piece again, playing Hungary and Yugoslavia for the first time.

Despite his avowed distaste for touring, Robert allowed himself this final trek though he refused to fly anywhere, worrying that, 'Flying is depersonalizing, we never get to see anything. Mainly though I object to being at the mercy of someone I'd probably hate in ordinary life.' To circumvent the problem, he insisted that all European travel should be by coach which turned the tour into one which lasted thirteen weeks, while they sailed across to America for that leg of the tour, picking up the tour bus there. Robert was clearly revelling in the company of the group, and in the absence of Lol Tolhurst. 'There hasn't been a scapegoat since he left which I know everyone worried about but now there's a lot more high-level, wordy sort of humour going on between everyone in the group and everyone's a fair target. They even take the piss out of me now . . . I think the group had outgrown him and the jokes are aimed at other people now. It's actually made everyone feel the way it used to, us against the world as against us picking on somebody in our midst. Without Lol, it's a different kind of tour, more draining – it would be stupid to be all jokey two minutes before going on stage and then go on and try to manufacture that kind of emotion.'

The concerts were simply riotous, the sets getting longer and longer, more and more dramatic and absorbingly powerful as the group neared the end, first in Europe and then in America. The dawning realization that perhaps Robert wasn't joking this time gave a manic element to the shows, everyone, fans and group alike, treating them as special events: 'I'm so set that when we come back from America that's it, that I know nothing in the world can change my mind. So each night when we're on stage I know we've got thirty-one concerts, seventy-four hours left or whatever. I'm actually counting down and each one gets progressively better because everyone's beginning to realize that I do mean it and it gives a real edge to the performances. I'd break my hands to avoid going out again.' Whether this was another shrewd mind-game that Smith was playing with himself and everyone else to enable the group to reach the heights night after night is something only he knows. And he's not telling.

The final UK shows were extraordinary, the last one itself, at Wembley Arena on July 24, lasting for very nearly four hours as the Cure leafed through their very extensive back catalogue, reaching a stage of near hysteria when it seemed as though they would never actually finish. Roger remarked, 'We argue about what songs to play because we want to play them all. We actually spend thousands in curfew fines because we want to play.' This time around, although the venues were as large as before, the Cure themselves did not need to pretend to be larger than life for the scale of the music had increased, the ferocity of their performance had increased, the frenetic reaction of the audience had increased and so the open spaces were adequately filled by that alone. The most important ingredient was probably supplied by the audiences themselves who, rather than coming to hear the pop songs, had come to see the Cure create their own atmosphere, to play what they wanted to play, but most of all to listen with the same dedication that they had when 'The Picture Tour' was making its way across the world back in 1981. This almost devotional setting and a wave of real feeling, an honest sense of regret that the Cure were going to finally leave the stage was tangible and it was an emotion that the group fed upon to produce their finest ever set of live performances.

When *Entreat*, effectively a concert version of *Disintegration*, finally came out a couple of years later in 1991 it was hailed as 'possibly the finest live album ever' by *Melody Maker*, a summing up that was hard to fault. Throughout 1989, the Cure were quite simply an awesome musical juggernaut that was unstoppable, such was the profound level of commitment in the group on every level. And yet, there was still time for disenchantment to enter the camp. Smith said, 'When we were in America last year, the concerts we played at the end of September, very soon after that there was a lot of conflict within the group just on that tour – the concerts were brilliant but the problems with touring have always been there. Because of the way the group is, because of the type of songs we play and the make-up within the group, it generally leads to a kind of excess on tour. Not excess in the rock 'n' roll sense but the feeling that you're there not only to perform as well as you can as if it's going to be your last concert, but also to experience everything as if it's your last day on earth. It tends to become very emotionally and physically exhausting. And as I get older, I find it takes me longer to recover . . . touring's not intrinsically tiring, it's what you make of it. Unfortunately when we're together, we encourage each other to excess, it becomes very wearing. It's also very gratifying but I'm just worried that we'll reach a point like so many bands where the concerts become secondary to actual touring. That's when the rot sets in.' More specifically, disagreements were beginning to flare up between Gallup and Williams on the one side and O'Donnell on the other. O'Donnell took to flying across the States between gigs while the others took the tour bus – this was O'Donnell's first taste of being a fully paid-up member of a group, having only ever worked as a session player previously, and he was clearly finding it difficult to adapt. He took his group duties seriously, however, and was 'trying to convince Robert to make the next album a dance project'.

Chapter Fourteen

NINETEEN NINETY was a year in which the Cure began to take some flak, not for their music but for their marketing approach. The third single to be drawn from *Disintegration* was 'Pictures Of You' in March and it came out in an astonishing ten formats, propelling it to No. 24 in the charts. It was released just prior to a BPI decree that allowed only four formats of any single. Understandably, hard-core Cure fans who had been building up their collection over the years were outraged by this crass commercial move, but worse was to come when, in the same month, the HMV chain offered a limited-edition promotional Cure CD and cassette entitled *Entreat* featuring eight songs from *Disintegration* recorded live at the Wembley concerts of the previous year. The catch was that to get a copy, you had to buy two Cure back-catalogue albums in the same format – to get *Entreat* on CD, you had to buy two old Cure CDs. Given that the Cure have a following as voracious in their collecting habits as any, this smacked of exploitation on the grand scale. Research has shown that, in the UK at least, Cure records sell an enormous proportion of their total sales within the first week of release, indicating that the core audience is fiercely loyal. A very large percentage of their audience has all the albums in their collection and so those people were less than delighted to be asked to buy the same records again in order to get what was an admittedly highly desirable Cure collectable.

The official line was that Smith had been talked into allowing the offer to go ahead, provided it was limited to France only, but over-zealous marketing had allowed it to cross the Channel. From the fans' point of view it was hard to know which was worse – if it had been available in France alone, they would still have been required to track it down via collectors' shops at extortionate prices while with it now being around in the UK, they felt ripped off when forced to buy product they already had.

Smith was dismayed at the outcome, shouldering part of the blame himself, upset that he hadn't fought harder to prevent it. 'The trouble is I give up . . . I think, "What is the fucking point of doing this?" then everyone rushes through this nonsense and then I think, "Oh no, I spent so many years making sure everything's right," and then I rush back into the fight again.'

With *Disintegration* finally wound up, the question for Cure fans everywhere was whether Robert would get the group together again, his pronouncements during that period having been none too encouraging. It was surprising, then, that in the spring of 1990 they met in a Sussex hotel to go through the new material that each had written, as had been the case prior to *Disintegration*. Smith had presumably anticipated further personnel difficulties given the upset at the end of the American tour and Roger's divergence from the group on the road and, sure enough, within a matter of hours, Simon and Boris on one side and Roger on the other were verbally attacking one another. Seeing that no compromise could be effected, Roger left the group, bringing the Cure down to a four-piece, something of a problem as they had already organized a series of festival dates across Europe, including Glastonbury in June and their own headlining show at the Crystal Palace Bowl in August.

Smith spent the next few weeks largely on the defensive, attempting to explain away this live activity, arguing that he'd never said he wouldn't play concerts again, just that he wouldn't tour and that this brief series of shows didn't constitute a tour, a pretty fine semantic line, though in christening the concerts 'Pleasure Trips', Smith tried to continue conveying the impression that this was just for his own amusement. Treading carefully, Porl intimated that, 'I think he just missed playing – he hasn't said too much and we haven't made a big deal out of it.' Simon was rather more forthright: 'The old bastard just wanted to do it again.' Eventually, Robert revealed, 'As long as we're making records we'll play live because otherwise it's just too solitary an experience.' The central problem now, with the first concerts looming, was who should play keyboards.

Given that the social element of the Cure is as important as the music, introducing new members to the band from outside had always been plagued with difficulties. This time, on Porl's suggestion, they decided to approach Perry Bamonte, who had been with their crew for six years, working especially closely with Robert. Since there was no problem on a personal level with him, he seemed to be the ideal choice, with one reservation as Bamonte, primarily a guitar player, explained at the time of his elevation. 'I've never played keyboards before in my life. I was going to take piano lessons but ironically touring with the Cure put paid to that.' Nevertheless, he was cajoled into taking over and spent days ensconced in Manor Studios playing along to the Cure's back catalogue in preparation for Glastonbury. Given his lack of rehearsal, he acquitted himself well and gained generally good reviews from the press.

While Perry was holed up learning his lines, the rest of the band were working on the ideas that they had brought to the fateful session when O'Donnell was dismissed. With O'Donnell now missing, it was ironic that his suggestion that the Cure should work on dance material was picked up, Robert feeling that if the group were ever to dip their feet into the electronic dance water, the summer of 1990 – the summer of Madchester – was the time to do it. In order to facilitate this move, rather than using Dave Allen to work on the tracks, dance producer and remixer Mark Saunders was called in to co-produce.

Sessions lasted for a considerable time, but Robert was generally dissatisfied with the outcome: 'We recorded about ten songs but because we've got a quality control that unfortunately a lot of bands don't have, we didn't release them just because we knew they'd sell. I genuinely wish that more groups would feel the same way about what they do but I know they won't.' Robert found an ally in this in Porl who was particularly upset that the group should be resorting to music made on machines, given the strong unified band approach that had run through the last couple of albums and *Disintegration* in particular. Porl and Boris had regularly worked together over the preceding couple of years, preparing music for the Cure, and their style lent heavily on that band sound, the absolute opposite to what the Cure were now trying to do. Eventually, Smith came to the conclusion that an out-and-out dance idiom was not one suited to the Cure and shelved all the material with the exception of 'Harold and Joe', Robert's delightfully ragged somnambulant vocal one of his most enjoyable performances for some time.

While the Cure were trying out their new songs, they did capture a piece, 'Never Enough', that caught the group spirit that Porl had been so jealously defending, the track coming together in the studio within a matter of an hour, based around a rhythm fragment from one of the early cassettes. It eventually featured some jaw-slackening guitar work from both Robert and Porl and an excitingly anguished vocal. Its only concession to the original purpose of the sessions was its use of the popular shuffle beat that was doing the indie-dance rounds at the time. This new song found its way into their live set immediately and justified its release as a one-off single later in the year.

'Never Enough', along with Perry's recruitment, turned the tide within the Cure from a group working almost exclusively in a keyboard-orientated framework to a loud guitar band, something that they hadn't toyed with for some little while. It was to be a further two years before that change bore fruit in the shape of a new record, but those summer concerts in 1990 certainly took on a different musical context, an interesting development since the song and its accompanying video drew on their live work. Smith opined, 'There is an obsessional aspect to the song because concerts are the new freak shows'. The video harked back to the darker side of Smith's psyche as 'Lullaby' had done previously. This time the Cure were shown playing live at an end-of-the-pier show, featuring various members and associates as freaks themselves, the band playing frantically within a tiny stage structure. Tim Pope saw the video as 'basically a documentary on the Cure. They're in their own little world built on this unstable structure.' Smith went further, saying, 'it's more vicious, about never feeling satisfied . . . it is like being stuck at the end of a pier sometimes. It was a play on how we could end up. I've seen other groups just acting things out on a small stage in front of a bunch of other freaks. I wear a ball and chain and when I fall towards the water, the thing that's holding me has saved me to put [me] through more years of hell.' It was a vivid depiction of one side of Smith's character, the hatred of going on tour fighting with the egotistical lure of live performance and the personal rush of feelings that it can generate.

Where Smith made his tactical error was to go on tour in the middle of the World Cup, 'Italia 90'. He ascribed this masochistic decision to his lack of faith in Bobby Robson's woeful England team, who somehow found their way to the semi-finals, and his belief that the early rounds would account for them – the tour would give him something else to think about instead. Naturally, the band ensured that there were televisions available at every show and that their contract made it clear that they would not go on stage until after the final game of the day had been played. The only difficulty came with their return to the Belgian Werchter festival, site of a fight with Robert Palmer's road crew nine years earlier. Bob Dylan was scheduled to top the bill at the festival which would have meant the Cure missing a game. 'I pulled my weight for once,' revealed Smith. 'I said, "unless we headline, I'm not going on". Somehow the promoter managed to convince Dylan that the really prestigious slot was second from top of the bill because everybody would be going to get the last train during the headliner's set, and he fell for it.' With all the critical arrangements in place, the Cure's shows were a revelation, not perhaps as fierce as those of the previous year, the atmosphere far lighter for much of the duration and all the more suited to festivals for that. They also gave weight to Robert's assertion that 'playing live has really helped to keep us from being pigeon-holed – the concerts can range from being really doom-laden to a night out in a weird disco.'

If the idea of writing dance-influenced songs had been indefinitely shelved, Smith still felt there might be possibilities for the Cure in that field given that previous releases had had some links to that musical area. The idea of a remix album was a fairly new one in 1990, though it has become increasingly popular since then as a great way of selling a record twice. Smith had been toying with releasing a second record in the mould of *Curiosity* to round up all the extended remixes that had featured on Cure singles over the years and which were now deleted and hard to find. 'I didn't want Cure fans to have to pay through the nose for collectable records.'

Once Robert reached the compilation stage, listening back to these early examples of the remixer's art, he began to have second thoughts about the idea since the results were not uniformly wonderful. 'They were awful, really dull. So it seemed pointless to just bring it out as a kind of archive thing and I thought we should use the opportunity to do something no one's done before. The record company weren't really aware of what we were doing until the whole thing was completed.' When the mixes began to stack up, Smith began to take stock of his idea: '"Lovecats" went to be mixed in New York with two supposedly very contemporary mixers – it was fucking dreadful. They managed to make it sound like a UB40 B-side. It was that bad. I put the first one that we got back on and I just sat there for about twenty minutes thinking, "What are we doing? What is this?" But as soon as I heard "Inbetween Days" I thought it was brilliant – exactly what we would never do as the Cure.'

Given his track record of presiding over virtually every aspect of the Cure's career, Robert's role in *Mixed Up* was odd, his involvement extending only as far as re-recording 'A Forest' and 'The Walk' with the rest of the group after the original master had disappeared. 'I thought if I got involved at all, it would just reduce the whole thing. I wanted people to remix the tracks as if it was just anyone.'

Allowing people, outsiders at that, to tamper with the Cure's music was something that the Smith of three or four years earlier would have found difficult to comprehend. *Mixed Up* is another staging post in the process of loosening his absolute grip on the group, lessening the emphasis on himself as the only voice in the Cure, and increasing the concentration on the music and on the other musicians rather than purely on him.

Perhaps it was a simple ruse to reduce the pressure on his shoulders or a genuine humility that has come with the realization that other people have valid ideas to contribute which may in turn help him to create better work in the future. There is also a case to be argued that, given the personal trials and tribulations that went into making *Disintegration*, Robert felt the need to do something lighter, to free himself from that emotional attachment to a record. He commented, 'I actually think it's very good. I've listened to it more than any other Cure album we've ever done because it sounds less like us than anything else and there's no emotional thing tugging at me when I hear any of the songs, all of the songs on it were less personal to me. This is the record that drunk Cure fans should listen to, it makes you feel really good, which is unusual for us.'

The reaction of fans was a factor that gave Robert his only real cause for concern, especially in the wake of the *Entreat* debacle. 'They might pre-judge it,' he confessed. 'Everyone should listen to it at least once – the only reason we've ever released anything is because it's musically very good. A small nucleus of fans just feel that certain old songs shouldn't be tampered with, but we're not that precious about it.' Smith has never been thrilled with the traditional whirl of promotional activity that surrounds record releases, but this time he threw himself into the fray more whole-heartedly, even setting up Cure FM as a private radio station during the evening of 31 August 1990 to alert people to the forthcoming record. Typically the entire event was a shambles – the station, housed in Fiction's offices, didn't manage to go on air until two in the morning, several hours late, but the band organized a second and far more successful stab at raising their own station a month later, each member playing songs of their own choice. Boris played the Sundays and the Chi-Lites, Perry went for Sisters of Mercy and Echo and the Bunnymen, Porl relied on the Beatles, Simon chose the Pixies and Tom Jones, and Robert played Bowie and the Only Ones. This entrepreneurial spirit must have been infectious for, a couple of years later, he became a director on the board of XFM, an indie-based radio station in London. Other odd projects continued throughout the rest of the year, including the recording of 'Hello I Love You' by the Doors for Elektra's anniversary album *Rubaiyat*, Elektra being the Cure's American label. Finally Robert turned up on Mark Goodier's Radio 1 show, ejecting the jock from the studio to open 'National Cure FM, Pirate Radio 1' as he kept reminding the listening nation. Sadly, it lasted just half an hour but he wasted little time in plugging *Mixed Up*, which peaked at No. 8. Critics were as nonplussed as some long-term fans, *Melody Maker* calling it 'extremely enjoyable' while *NME* described it as 'very patchy' and a 'negative statement'.

Further promotion came in the shape of the single release of the remixed 'Close To Me'. Smith was dubious about its merits, saying, 'I've never been that comfortable with all that promoting an album with a single, particularly when the single's already been out once. And they wanted to marry it to the old video because it saves money, so I said that it definitely wouldn't come out without a new video . . . I suppose the difference is they're all trying to sell records and I'm not because we sell enough, far more than I ever thought we would.' Pope's new Cure video picked up from the original with the wardrobe falling from the cliff. It was similar to his recent work on 'Suboceana' for Tom Tom Club and returned to the enjoyment theme after the more perversely comic 'Never Enough'.

Ad hoc activities continued to take up the group's time for the next few months, the new year opening with a flurry of work that was filmed as *The Cure Play Out* for later video release. This included a warm-up concert at London's T&C2, when they were billed as Five Imaginary Boys. Some of the concert was broadcast on BBC2's *Snub TV*, including a couple of new songs which the band had just finished recording. Plans had been laid to release these as an EP but Robert felt that it might be misinterpreted as there was no new album scheduled to go with it. There followed an evening as the house band on Jonathan Ross's show, and a classic appearance on MTV's *Unplugged*, over which Robert admitted to an outbreak of nerves. The show was one of the best of that series, the group joining in with the spirit of the ideas, furnishing the audience with kazoos for 'The Walk' and playing toy pianos, unlike other artists who eschew electric guitars and bring in a fifteen-piece band to create a similarly huge sound. *Unplugged* was a nice summation of their prevailing spirit of mischievous fun though their performance at the BPI Brit Awards reminded all and sundry that there was still plenty of spleen-venting left to be done as Robert branded the awards ceremony a farce and the Cure produced an explosive version of 'Never Enough'.

The Cure picked up the 'Best Band' gong for 1990 – odd considering their only work that year had been a couple of live shows, and the release of *Mixed Up*. Smith was incensed that the Cure had been used merely to lend credibility to an otherwise appalling show with an equally horrendous past by playing the Great British Music Weekend in January. Having been assured that on the night itself all those performing would be playing live, the Cure were the only group to do so, while almost every other award winner failed to turn up. To round the evening off, Robert thanked every member of the Cure past and present with the exception of Lol Tolhurst, clearly indicating their displeasure with Lol's attacks on the Cure while doing press to launch his new group Presence. The band were particularly upset since, in an attempt to help out and bury the hatchet between the two parties, Porl had played guitar on Presence's debut single 'In Wonder'.

To round off this current batch of business, *Entreat* was given a little-publicized release in March 1991 to appease Cure fans who still didn't have the record, though the decision to put it in a different-coloured sleeve was not designed to please collectors. Unwilling to gain from this mess, the Cure gave royalties to Amnesty International, Mencap, NSPCC, cot death research and the Doctor Hadwen Trust For Humane Research. And finally, in June, *Picture Show* was released collecting together all the videos the Cure had done since *Staring at the Sea*, along with home-movie-style footage illustrating the lengths to which Lol had been victimized during his tenure, Robert taking malicious glee in parodying his keyboard style.

Not since 1983 had the Cure been involved in so many diverse and seemingly strange projects, but this was not entirely coincidental, as Robert revealed. 'After we did *Pornography* we followed it up with three of the most stupid songs we've ever done and after *Disintegration* we would have been forced internally to do something superficial but this has taken care of that side of things.' The group were free to take whatever direction they chose when sessions began in the summer of 1991 to prepare a new album, the first to feature the current line-up and this new more buoyant frame of mind. The only cloud on the horizon was the news in July that Lol had decided to take legal action against Robert and Chris Parry for a greater share of past royalties.

The new record, with the working title *Higher*, was made at a residential studio once again, Shipton Manor in Oxfordshire. Again, they had taken time to come up with a sizeable backlog of material, Perry Bamonte joining in this time. 'We all wrote things at home and brought them together before recording,' he commented. Robert revealed: 'We demoed more than forty songs altogether and the way the album finally comes out depends on which of those we concentrate on. In the end there were sixteen real possibles but we can only have twelve because of the time restrictions on the length of the CD.' One had survived from the putative EP from 1991, 'A Letter To Elise', which was worked on further, the rest emerging from demos.

Most noticeable was the completely different atmosphere to that which had prevailed at the time of *Disintegration*. Robert said, 'When we've been apart from each other for a long time and we meet up with all our new songs, it's exciting. I get a real buzz out of getting in the van with this lot again, and when we first came to the studio we were out on our mountain bikes around the countryside or getting down to the pub at the end of the field. An enormous part of why we're together is based on the fact that we're socially compatible. Within the group, the whole atmosphere's been better, more fun, more enjoyable.' Much of this new feeling was put down to the absence of Lol – 'An irritant, we all despised him but now everyone's here for the right reasons' according to Smith – and the arrival of Perry, Porl noting the 'much freer atmosphere' since he'd joined the group. Chris Parry felt that, 'Simon's a close mate of Robert's, obviously – but that's more like a "lads together" friendship. Perry's in tune with Robert on a cerebral plane.' Robert admitted, 'During *Disintegration* I could switch myself off from everyone else. Now it'd be impossible. Now everybody's involved not just in the atmosphere but in contributing to the songs down to the last detail. In the old days I wouldn't let people do certain things because it didn't seem to work, it didn't seem to fit in with the whole. In Porl's case particularly, I've inhibited some of the things maybe he would have wanted to do on past records but it's reached the point where the whole thing feels so much more like a real group now.'

Indeed, so happy were they at the Manor that they turned it into their own home, Robert saying towards the end of their time there, 'We feel really bitter about the next group coming in. It's our house.' The home comforts had a derogatory effect on this record according to some, *RCD* seeing it as an album of consolidation, 'pure Cure and few surprises at a point where surprises would prove to be too dangerous'. *Melody Maker* agreed that 'the Cure have never sounded better. *Nothing* has ever sounded better.' *NME*, however, termed it an 'astonishing record'. The atmosphere was conducive to writing and recording, for at one time it seemed likely that the Cure would come up with two new albums, one of which was to be instrumental. 'It started because Porl had written an excellent weird thing,' explained Smith. 'Very stirring, with bagpipes and harmonium which he really wanted to do but it didn't fit any of the lyrics I'd been writing. Simon had a piece too which is nominally called "Off To Sleep", a nursery rhyme kind of sound, very sweet and gentle but if I tried to sing over it, it would get very morose. So we hit on the idea of a separate album of purely instrumental things . . . the fifth one sounded like a Cure backing track without me singing. That seemed a bit pointless so we shelved it for the moment but we'll probably get back to it.' Robert later told the American press that the next album would be an instrumental.

In fact, Robert chose to clear the decks of these songs in November 1994. The Cure released a limited edition cassette available only by mail order direct from Fiction. Entitled *Lost Wishes*, it comprised four pieces, 'Uyea Sound', 'Cloudberry', 'Off To Sleep . . .' and 'The Three Sisters'. The selection was remixed by Robert and offered for sale in order to benefit the Portsmouth Down's Syndrome Trust. Its release also prevented Smith having to answer any further questions as to the fate of the instrumentals when he was more interested in the next album. Also, given that Porl and Boris had both left by this time, it made little sense to add further instrumentals to four pieces made two years earlier by a totally different line-up. The 1992 album, eventually entitled *Wish*, took diversity as its theme in the same way *The Head On The Door* had, the linking element being the keenness to utilize the guitar far more. 'Everyone played out a bit more,' Robert admitted. 'We had in mind the way it feels live to play as a guitar band, it's so much more exciting.' The album was more raucous at times than much of their recent material, but it still succeeded in covering a tremendous amount of emotional ground. 'To Wish Impossible Things' was an admission that, 'In all relationships, there are always aching holes and that's where the impossible wishes come into it.' 'Apart' was melancholic and ruminative, 'From The Edge Of The Deep Green Sea' was an epic underpinned by some superb drumming, 'Cut' a scathingly violent diatribe that could possibly have been taken as another stab at Lol, and 'Open' a meditation on the wonders and otherwise of drink. In the midst of this powerful soul-baring were some astounding pop songs, 'Doing The Unstuck' about Robert's favourite subject of escapism, 'High' was Smith at his most sticky, sickly sweet and 'Friday I'm In Love' quite the most exuberant thing they've ever done, Robert likening it to '"Boys Don't Cry", that old-fashioned Beatles craft of the perfect pop song'. The latter two were both singles, the first featuring a video that was apparently based on Terry Gilliam's film *Brazil*, the second a drunken knees-up that had a similar feel to 'Inbetween Days' almost a decade earlier.

The song which provoked the most controversy was 'End' which appeared to be Robert Smith attempting to shy away from his audience, rejecting those personae that had been projected onto him and looking for a way out. Far more than anything from *Disintegration*, 'End' sounded as if this might really be the final song from the final album. Smith demurred, explaining, 'In one sense, it's me addressing myself. It's about the persona I sometimes fall into. On another level, it's addressed to people who expect me to know things and have answers, and it has a broader idea, to do with the way you fall into a path, it just becomes habitual even though it's not really the way you want to be . . . I had it in the back of my mind when I wrote the song that when it comes to performing on the tour, it would remind me each night that I'm not reducible to what I'm doing. I do need reminding because it's got to the stage where I could quite happily fall into the rock star trap . . . our success has reached the kind of magnitude where it's insistent and insidious.'

Smith is sometimes placed in an impossible position by his fans, as Andrew Mueller's *Melody Maker* article detailing the Cure's American tour in 1992 illustrates. Stephen Sweet, the photographer with Mueller, was approached by two fans who ascertained he would be meeting the group. They then gave him a photo to give to Robert. It was of a friend, a big Cure fan, who had been killed in a car crash the year before. 'When Smith's given the photo,' wrote Mueller, 'he looks totally at a loss. Eventually he borrows a pen, scrawls "what can I possibly write?" across the top of it and signs his name to the bottom.' Given that fans expect him to be a seer and a sage, it's barely surprising that he's gone off the rails a few times and is so keen to surround himself with people who are empathetic without taking him or themselves too seriously. 'People [are] waiting for me and the Cure to stand for something. All that nearly drove me around the bend. And I don't need any encouragement.'

Yet still Smith rails at the level of success he has achieved, having 'a feeling of wanting to break away from what I'm doing with which I'm very comfortable. I think maybe I should do something I don't feel confident about, to try and get back that sense of danger. But then I wonder if I really miss that danger. Do I really want to sacrifice my happiness for the chance of experiencing more, when I've already jeopardized my entire life many times just for the sake of experiencing things?'

It was that kind of desire to reach for extremes that contributed to the decision to embark on another world tour in support of *Wish*, the Cure playing a series of smaller UK dates in April 1992 to warm up for the larger venues that lay ahead. Sailing into New York on the *QE2*, they arrived to find that *Wish* had debuted on the *Billboard* chart at No. 2, having gone in at No. 1 in the UK, far and away their greatest success to date. 'I had decided to do less,' agreed Robert, 'the whole thing was really draining me. But we sat down and decided how much we enjoyed it.' The new group spirit contributed to Smith's decision but so did the audiences who, Smith felt, had listened more on the previous tour and to whom he was beginning to feel some allegiance, a massive petition from Australia actually getting him onto a plane again. Even so, 'I have mixed feelings about going on tour again,' Smith revealed. 'I worry about the effect it's gonna have on everyone, I really do. I can see it being like last time only multiplied because of what the group is now. I can see it being more intense onstage . . . you run the risk of it all merging into this world of hyper-reality but that intensity is a big feeling. It's not easy to throw that away,' a sentiment he echoed when commenting, 'I've started to miss playing live, which is worrying.'

Nevertheless, the Cure made it round the world generally unscathed although Simon missed some European dates when he was taken ill with pleurisy. The concerts were impressive events though they seemed to lack some of the passionate grandeur that had made the *Disintegration* shows so memorable. Inevitably, as the band reached the end of the road, Robert reiterated that as far as touring was concerned, it literally was the end of the road. This time it all seemed more believable even if it was only prompted by the difficulties that the tail-end of the itinerary had bestowed on them with Simon's disappearance.

For Porl at least, there would be no more tours for, for the second time, he chose to leave the group. There were no ill feelings, but as Robert noted, 'Even at the start of 1992 I knew he wanted to leave. He just wanted to do different things really . . . he tends to do things on his own. We have a lot in common and a lot in uncommon as well. Porl likes different music to us but it's really good because the side of the group that I've encouraged, like having solos and getting a lot heavier, a lot of that's actually Porl's influence. He restrains himself and does what's best for the group but if he was left to his own devices, he'd play guitar solos over everything. He actually does in the studio. We let him play over everything and then we just don't use it in the mix. We record it, then make ten copies where his guitars are blindingly loud.' It wasn't too much of a shock then when a shaven-headed Porl turned up with Robert Plant and Jimmy Page for the 'Unledded' project in 1994.

Given the close relationship he enjoyed with Porl, and following a couple of interviews towards the end of the *Wish* tour that suggested he was looking for more challenges, it was perhaps no surprise when Boris chose to quit the band too, though this revelation wasn't made public until the release of the 'Lost Wishes' cassette in November 1994. It's likely though that this decision was made much earlier but kept under wraps until the local battle with Lol Tolhurst was over.

Thompson's swan-song with the Cure came with the release of 1993's cinema film *Show*, though by this time the four-piece Cure had played at the Great Xpectations show in Finsbury Park, London, in aid of XFM, finding their way onto a live album from the event. *Show* was directed by Aubrey Powell, who directed for Paul McCartney in the same summer, and he produced an excellent concert package. Sadly though, he did not produce a Cure film and so *Show* scarcely stood out from the stampeding herds of concert films that clog the shelves of the HMV shops nationwide. 'We were cajoled into sacrificing Tim Pope's imagination for someone else's workmanship abilities,' Smith observed. 'I really wish we'd used him, it would have been a much better film.' Taking over the editing, Smith made 350 changes in a week but was happy about the move from a sepia-tinted crowd into the full colour of the group, à la *The Wizard Of Oz*. 'The whole idea for the colour was portraying that sort of magical world that was almost unreal, like hyper-real and I thought of introducing us as characters because, despite ourselves, it's very difficult not to ham when there's a camera around.' The film came about because, 'Every time anywhere in the world they show us in concert it's *The Cure In Orange* and it's so unrepresentative it makes me want to cry.' Lol's presence in that film is also a pretty potent reason why Smith wants it expunged from his memory. A double live CD soundtrack was released too but, recognizing that the track listing was not entirely representative of the band's catalogue, being fairly uptempo, the Cure also released *Paris*, another, superior, live record which featured the harder edge of their by now extensive repertoire. Since *Show* came out in October 1993, the Cure have maintained a low profile, contributing to the soundtrack of the ill-fated Brandon Lee film *The Crow*. Their main preoccupation however – at least for Smith and Parry – has been defending themselves against a legal action brought by Lol Tolhurst in which he argued for the setting aside of a 1986 agreement which reduced his status in the Cure from an equal footing with Robert to a lower royalty percentage, though one which still exceeded that of the rest of the group. Tolhurst alleged that he was badly advised at the time and that Smith and Parry had deliberately pressurized him into signing this new contract. The case was inevitably messy and bitter, rehearsing many of the arguments as to Tolhurst's musical validity which have already been highlighted in this book.

Although the case was opened in February, it wasn't until 16 September that Mr Justic Chadwick delivered judgment in the High Court of Justice, Chancery Division. In a written ruling, the judge noted that Robert Smith was clearly the chief songwriter and musician in the group and that there were no grounds for him to presume that Tolhurst had not signed the contract of his own free will, intimating that given his 'very serious problems with alcohol addiction from which he might have hoped to recover, but which were, at the time, severely limiting his ability to perform as a musician', Tolhurst had in fact been fortunate to come out of the 1986 deal so well. The judge further noted that the other members of the group had expressed their dismay at Lol's elevated position in the band compared with their own status.

The case clearly left some scars but it remained for Chris Parry to issue the official line. 'The Cure have always been about music although, clearly, a lot of money has been made. It was a most painful and distressing experience to be dragged into court on money matters and one can only hope this judgment may precipitate a growth in Laurence Tolhurst's spiritual development.' Lol chose not to appeal against the decision and a later hearing will decide on who should bear the estimated £1,000,000 legal costs. Robert's reaction was not placed on record but immediate plans were laid for the Cure to start recording a new album in October 1994, without Porl or Boris. No replacement have been sought at the time of writing.

As an antidote to the serious business in court, Robert did make a surprise appearance on BBC's 'alternative ' comedy show *Newman & Baddiel In Pieces* in late 1993, a response to their lampooning of Smith in earlier episodes of its forerunner *The Mary Whitehouse Experience*, where their version of the Cure were to be seen droning their way though such favourites as 'The Laughing Policeman'. In this rare TV appearance, Robert led a conga through a graveyard, a fitting metaphor on which to end, for hasn't he been doing that for the last twenty years?

Chapter Fifteen

MUCH OF this book has concerned itself with that great intangible, 'atmosphere'. That the Cure have created their own unique musical environment is so self-evident by now that it needs little further comment and yet that is not the central issue in the career of Robert Smith. Smith's working life, one dedicated to escapism in one form or another, is a life spent in pursuit of the ideal, possibly idealized working environment; the creation and propagation of a working unit that renders him immune to the world outside, allowing him to continue to function within his own universe of which he is unashamedly the centre. Contrary to popular myth Robert Smith is trying to escape the doom, gloom and despondency – the Cure is his means to that end: 'I still feel that ultimately everything is really futile, everything I do is really meaningless. The band takes my mind off things, it makes me feel happier.'

Down the years, Smith has pursued that end single-mindedly but by very, very different methods. His leadership of the Cure has varied from the benign to the fascistic and back again, from the seizing of an almost absolute state of domination to the stage it has reached today where, although he is the chairman of the Cure's board with the casting vote, he is no longer prepared simply to use his strategic power to get his way but will openly accept and digest criticism and new ideas from those who he trusts: Simon Gallup, and Perry Bamonte.

Robert's adoption of the democratic way indicates just how much he has changed as a person over the course of the Cure's career and how much the other personalities within the group have adapted or been replaced. Smith has matured as far as his relationships with people are concerned, accepting that to get the best from others, he has to be willing to listen, though with the instincts of the ruthless football manager he has never worried about chopping and changing the side to achieve the perfect blend. He is, like anyone else, a paradox – you could not help but like the man who wrote the lyrics to 'Lovesong' yet at the same time you'd feel wary of the guy that wrote 'Disintegration'. Sometimes he can be accused of throwing a lyrical tantrum which can be frightening and amusing at the same time, and it is a facet of Robert Smith's work which has to be accepted for it is the flip-side of the childish innocence and wonder that has kept the Cure afloat and made them so astonishingly appealing.

To paraphrase one of Robert's contemporaries, the Cure are stars and they shine so hard. In a musical world which is increasingly faceless and devoid of personality, mirroring as it should, indeed must, the world around it, the Cure stand out like diamonds in the dirt – rough ones perhaps, but diamonds none the less. Robert Smith understands what it is to be a pop star and what the role demands. After all, he claims to have retained the mentality of a thirteen-year-old, the age at which we want stars, when we look up to the great and glamorous. If a punk in some of his attitudes, Smith has not perpetuated the myth that anyone and everyone can be a pop star and that the audience is the same as the performer, just six feet lower. He has rejected this for the palpable nonsense that it is. Robert Smith is a pop star and manipulates that status to his advantage, toys with it for as long as it engages him but is always willing to complain about it and return to the island of the sensitive artist when the pressures become too intrusive.

For Robert Smith is an artist too, an interesting, often fascinating one who has been able to create some of the finest introspective music of the age, drawing on his own reality to illuminate universal themes. His sheltered world has enabled him to dedicate himself to his art form, as has been the case of many writers throughout history. If Smith were not there, where else would we look within popular music for the expression of such universal themes?

That Robert Smith has been determinedly selfish throughout the history of the Cure is apparent. It is this characteristic that has brought him such acclaim – he had the vision to realize that other people would comprehend the topics he chose to tackle and would appreciate the lack of flippancy in dealing with those subjects. Coupled with the moments of lighter relief that have come later, it is a vision not shared by many. Other members of the group have necessarily had to share that vision or they would not be able to take any part in Robert's world, and yet their selfishness has had to be tempered, at least until recently, to avoid treading on Smith's artistic toes. Simon Gallup, Robert's closest friend, went into exile until he was able to formulate a way of working with Smith at close quarters. The passing of time has inevitably made it easier for each to tolerate the other's quirks too, as have the greater financial rewards which make life for the itinerant musician a far more comfortable experience. That said, Smith appears to have finally hit on the perfect team both musically and personally, the escape route for him to use when assailed by the demons that periodically surround him. Team-work, up to a point, is now the watchword.

Much has been made here of the contribution of Tim Pope. It has to be said that Tim Pope is not the shadowy figure behind the Cure's success. What is demonstrable is that Pope was a catalyst for Smith's decision to take a look at his method of working, reappraise it and change it to embrace the contributions and therefore the trust and affection of the others in the group. Pope's status as an artistic equal cannot be questioned for it was his imagination and technical ability that provided Robert with the tools to desert his doom-laden past. It was, however, Robert Smith who used those tools, reinventing himself – but perhaps reinventing is too strong a word, for the character in 'Let's Go To Bed' was always there; he just needed to be given the opportunity to liberate himself.

Smith has changed as a person, but he has not grown up, a point he would make most forcibly. Pope would agree: 'I saw them in America at the Dodgers Stadium in front of 59,000 people and I thought, "Fucking hell, Smith's still moaning about the same old crap," which is what he does. He just stands there and moans and wails quite a lot, but I love the fact that he's just totally obsessed with the same things all the time, all these recurrent images, "push" and "rejection", the claustrophobia. It's great to see someone who carries straight on like that without letting fashion influence him. Robert still wears the same jumper he had at school, he never essentially changes, he just develops.'

For a group tagged so remorselessly as representing the gothic school of funereal dirges, the Cure have embraced an incredible range of music for Smith has never been slow to exercise his prerogative to do what he wants, how he wants and when he wants. That development has been critical too, for though he has remained true to the same lyrical ideas through his career, he has found myriad methods of expressing them, putting them within the most unlikely settings. The question is now for how much longer can it go on? Smith has attempted to shed the lost teddy bear side of his image of late but with the same preoccupations it is hard to envisage him on stage at forty – yet this is not necessarily because Smith will appear ridiculous as a forty-year-old innocent but because we as a culture are totally unprepared for the spectacle. It may be that he will discover a way to overcome the hurdle though in sheer physical terms it's a daunting one, but it is more likely that by that stage the Cure will have ceased to be a functioning live group, retiring to the studio instead.

For one who is always so conscious of the passing of time and how fleeting life is, Robert Smith has made remarkably few studio albums, just ten in his career, if *Japanese Whispers* is accepted, and only four in the last ten years. Perhaps he feels that he has said all there is to say, but more likely it proves that he has achieved a degree of balance in his life between the personal and the professional. The indications are that Robert enjoys both facets of his life and, given his financial security, has chosen to enjoy that in the company of friends and family. It is only when he is stricken by emotional turmoil or the need to play again that he is tempted back to the studio. Cure fans might like Robert to be more productive but, viewed objectively, they would have to concede that he has created an ideal way of life for himself and wish him good luck with it.

Objectivity is one of the things lacking in the Cure's music and this is a criticism often thrown at them. Yet what makes objectivity such a laudable aim? Robert Smith clearly lives within his songs, they come from the heart and express his feelings in what for him is a lucid manner which is all he has ever really tried to do, though later records suggest an attempt to shed the ambiguity. Even when his lyrics are impenetrable, there is still the music which always conveys the emotion of the song and, at worst, his words are interesting and sometimes funny. Those for whom they strike a particular chord are invited to live inside the songs to such an extent that the Cure have the largest die-hard cult following within their audience of any band of comparable size.

It is Smith's refusal to accept any lyrical compromise which prevents him gaining access to the pantheon of greats whenever music critics compile their lists. *Pornography* and *Faith*, for instance, are dismissed as 'difficult' or 'flawed' when to Smith they are as they should be, expressions of his feelings at the time. When the history books on popular music are rewritten in the next century, the Cure will have earned their entry, but it is likely to be as a pop group that they are remembered. This is not surprising if you consider the compilation tape you could make of their music: 'Boys Don't Cry', 'Friday I'm In Love', 'Inbetween Days', 'Lullaby.', 'Why Can't I Be You?', 'Catch', 'High', 'Never Enough', 'Lovesong', 'The Caterpillar', 'Close To Me', 'Pictures Of You', 'Killing An Arab', 'The Lovecats'. That list goes on and on and makes one of the finest singles collection since the Beatles *Red* and *Blue* albums. But that is to overlook the power and glory of 'Disintegration', 'The Figurehead', 'Faith', 'One Hundred Years', 'The Kiss', 'End', 'In Your House', 'Pornography', 'The Same Deep Water As You', 'The Holy Hour' or 'Untitled'.

If you look back over pop history, there have been few people who deserve the word 'genius' – John Lennon, Jimi Hendrix, possibly Syd Barrett. Robert Smith is capable of taking a place in that company. Genius, after all, does not imply consistency for that is the attribute of the talented journeyman. A genius, as the dictionary defines, it is 'a person with an exceptional ability, especially of a highly original kind'. Some of his songs have meant little or nothing to anyone but himself, some have been sufficiently broad to have a universal appeal. In the company of his friends, he's made some great records and some that do not translate. But they have all been exceptional in some way and they have all been highly original. Draw your own conclusions.

UK Discography

Singles

KILLING AN ARAB
10:15 Saturday Night
Small Wonder Records, December 1978

KILLING AN ARAB
10:15 Saturday Night
Fiction Records, February 1979

BOYS DON'T CRY
Plastic Passion
Fiction Records, June 1979

JUMPING SOMEONE ELSE'S TRAIN
I'm Cold
Fiction Records, November 1979

A FOREST
Another Journey By Train
Fiction Records, April 1980
Chart Position: 31

PRIMARY
Primary (extended version), Descent
Fiction Records, May 1981
Chart Position: 43

CHARLOTTE SOMETIMES
Splintered In Her Head, Faith (live)
Fiction Records, October 1981
Chart Position: 44

THE HANGING GARDEN
One Hundred Years, Killing An Arab (live), A Forest (live)
Fiction Records, July 1982
Chart Position: 34

LET'S GO TO BED
Just One Kiss, Let's Go To Bed (extended version),
Just One Kiss (extended version)
Fiction Records, November 1982
Chart Position: 44

THE WALK
The Upstairs Room, The Dream, La Ment
Fiction Records, July 1983
Chart Position: 12

THE LOVECATS
Speak My Language, The Lovecats (extended version), Mr Pink
   Eyes
Fiction Records, October 1983
Chart Position: 7

THE CATERPILLAR
Happy The Man, Throw Your Foot
Fiction Records, April 1984
Chart Position: 14

INBETWEEN DAYS
The Exploding Boy, A Few Hours After This
Fiction Records, July 1985
Chart Position: 15

CLOSE TO ME (REMIX)
A Man Inside My Mouth, Close To Me (extended version), New
    Day, Stop Dead
Fiction Records, September 1985
Chart Position: 24

BOYS DON'T CRY (NEW VOICE MIX)
Pillbox Tales, Boys Don't Cry (New Voice Club Mix), Do The
    Hansa
Fiction Records, April 1986
Chart Position: 22

WHY CAN'T I BE YOU?
A Japanese Dream, Six Different Ways (live), Push (live), Why
    Can't I Be You? (remix), A Japanese Dream (remix)
Fiction Records, April 1987
Chart Position: 21

CATCH
Breathe, Kyoto Song (live), A Night Like This (live), A Chain Of
    Flowers
Fiction Records, June 1987
Chart Position: 27

JUST LIKE HEAVEN (REMIX)
Snow In Summer, Sugar Girl
Fiction Records, October 1987
Chart Position: 29

HOT HOT HOT!!! (REMIX)
Hot Hot Hot!!! (extended remix), Hey You!!! (extended remix)
Fiction Records, February 1988
Chart Position: 45

PEEL SESSIONS EP
Killing An Arab, 10:15 Saturday Night, Fire In Cairo, Boys Don't
    Cry
Strange Fruit Records, May 1988

LULLABY (REMIX)
Babble, Out Of Mind, Lullaby (extended remix)
Fiction Records, April 1989
Chart Position: 5

LOVESONG (7" MIX)
2 Late, Lovesong (extended mix), Fear Of Ghosts
Fiction Records, August 1989
Chart Position: 18

PICTURES OF YOU (REMIX)
Last Dance (live), Fascination Street (live), Prayers For Rain (live),
    Disintegration (live), Pictures Of You (extended remix)
Fiction Records, March 1990
Chart Position: 24

NEVER ENOUGH
Harold And Joe, Let's Go To Bed (Milk Mix), Never Enough (Big
    Mix)
Fiction Records, September 1990
Chart Position: 13

CLOSE TO ME (CLOSEST MIX)
Just Like Heaven (Dizzy Mix), Primary (Red Mix), Close To Me,
    (Closer Mix), Why Can't I Be You? (extended mix)
Fiction Records, October 1990
Chart Position: 13

HIGH
This Twilight Garden, Play, High (Higher Mix)
Fiction Records, March 1992
Chart Position: 8

HIGH (TRIP MIX)
Open (Fix Mix)
Fiction Records, April 1992
Chart Position: 44

FRIDAY I'M IN LOVE
Halo, Scared As You, Friday I'm In Love (Strangelove Mix)
Fiction Records, May 1992
Chart Position: 6

A LETTER TO ELISE
The Big Hand, A Foolish Arrangement, A Letter To Elise (Blue Mix)
Fiction Records, 1992
Chart Position: 28

Compact Disc Videos

CLOSE TO ME (VIDEO)
Close To Me (12″ mix), A Man Inside My Mouth, Stop Dead, New Day
Fiction Records, August 1987

WHY CAN'T I BE YOU? (VIDEO)
A Japanese Dream, Hey You!!!, Why Can't I Be You?
Fiction Records, October 1988

INBETWEEN DAYS (VIDEO)
Six Different Ways (live), Push (live)
Fiction Records, October 1988

CATCH (VIDEO)
Catch, Breathe, A Chain Of Flowers, Icing Sugar (New Mix)
Fiction Records, October 1988

Albums

THREE IMAGINARY BOYS
10.15 Saturday Night / Accuracy / Grinding Halt / Another Day / Object / Subway Song / Foxy Lady / Meathook / So What / Fire In Cairo / It's Not You / Three Imaginary Boys
Fiction Records, May 1979
Chart Position: 44

SEVENTEEN SECONDS
A Reflection / Play For Today / Secrets / In Your House / Three /
  The Final Sound / A Forest / M / At Night / Seventeen Seconds
Fiction Records, April 1980
Chart Position: 20

FAITH
The Holy Hour / Primary / Other Voices / All Cats Are Grey / The
  Funeral Party / Doubt / The Drowning Man / Faith
(Cassette versions include 'Carnage Visors')
Fiction Records, April 1981
Chart Position: 14

PORNOGRAPHY
One Hundred Years / A Short Term Effect / The Hanging Garden /
  Siamese Twins / The Figurehead / A Strange Day / Pornography
Fiction Records, May 1982
Chart Position: 8

BOYS DON'T CRY
Boys Don't Cry / Plastic Passion / 10.15 Saturday Night / Accuracy /
  So What / Jumping Someone Else's Train / Subway Song / Killing
  An Arab / Fire In Cairo / Another Day / Grinding Halt / Three
  Imaginary Boys
Fiction Records, August 1983
(Originally released in USA in November 1979)
Chart Position: 71

JAPANESE WHISPERS
Let's Go to Bed / Just One Kiss / The Dream / The Upstairs Room /
  The Walk / La Ment / Speak My Language / The Lovecats
Fiction Records, December 1983
Chart Position: 26

THE TOP
Shake Dog Shake / Bird Mad Girl / Wailing Wall / Give Me It /
  Dressing Up / The Caterpillar / Piggy In The Mirror / The
  Empty World / Bananafishbones / The Top
Fiction Records, May 1984
Chart Position: 10

CONCERT

Shake Dog Shake / Primary / Charlotte Sometimes / The Hanging Garden / Give Me It / The Walk / One Hundred Years / A Forest / 10.15 Saturday Night / Killing An Arab

Cassette version includes CURIOSITY: Heroin Face / Boys Don't Cry / Subway Song / At Night / In Your House / The Drowning Man / Other Voices / The Funeral Party / All Mine / Forever (version)

Fiction Records, October 1984

Chart Position: 26

THE HEAD ON THE DOOR

Inbetween Days / Kyoto Song / The Blood / Six Different Ways / Push / The Baby Screams / Close To Me / A Night Like This / Screw / Sinking

Fiction Records, August 1985

Chart Position: 7

STANDING ON A BEACH – THE SINGLES

Killing An Arab / 10.15 Saturday Night / Boys Don't Cry / Jumping Someone Else's Train / A Forest / Play For Today / Primary / Other Voices / Charlotte Sometimes / The Hanging Garden / Let's Go to Bed / The Walk / The Lovecats / The Caterpillar / Inbetween Days / Close To Me / A Night Like This

Cassette version includes THE UNAVAILABLE B-SIDES: I'm Cold / Another Journey By Train / Descent / Splintered In Her Head / Mr Pink Eyes / Happy The Man / Throw Your Foot / The Exploding Boy / A Few Hours After This / A Man Inside My Mouth / Stop Dead / New Day

Fiction Records, May 1986

Chart Position: 4

KISS ME KISS ME KISS ME

The Kiss / Catch / Torture / If Only Tonight We Could Sleep / Why
Can't I Be You? / How Beautiful You Are / Snakepit / Hey You!!! /
Just Like Heaven / All I Want / Hot Hot Hot!!! / One More Time /
Like Cockatoos / Icing Sugar / The Perfect Girl / A Thousand
Hours / Shiver And Shake / Fight.
CD version excludes Hey You!!!
Fiction Records, May 1987
Chart Position: 6

KISS ME KISS ME KISS ME

The above album was released with an additional limited edition
mini-album on orange vinyl: A Japanese Dream / Breathe / Chain
Of Flowers / Sugar Girl / Snow In Summer / Icing Sugar / Shake
Dog Shake / Primary / Charlotte Sometimes
Fiction Records, December 1987

DISINTEGRATION

Plainsong / Pictures Of You / Closedown / Lovesong / Last Dance /
Lullaby / Fascination Street / Prayers For Rain / The Same Deep
Water As You / Disintegration / Homesick / Untitled
LP version excludes Last Dance and Homesick
Fiction Records, May 1989
Chart Position: 3

MIXED UP

Lullaby (Extended Mix) / Close To Me (Closer Mix) / Fascination
Street (Extended Mix) / The Walk (Everything Mix) / Lovesong
(Extended Mix) / A Forest (Tree Mix) / Pictures Of You
(Extended Mix) / Hot Hot Hot!!! (Extended Mix) / Why Can't I
Be You? (Extended Mix) / The Caterpillar (Flicker Mix) /
Inbetween Days (Shiver Mix) / Never Enough (Big Mix)
CD Version excludes Why Can't I Be You? (Extended Mix)
Fiction Records, November 1990
Chart Position: 8

ENTREAT

Pictures Of You / Closedown / Last Dance / Fascination Street /
Prayers For Rain / Disintegration / Homesick / Untitled
Fiction Records, March 1991
Chart Position: 10

WISH

Open / High / Apart / From the Edge Of The Deep Green Sea /
Wendy Time / Doing The Unstuck / Friday I'm In Love / Trust /
A Letter To Elise / Cut / To Wish Impossible Things / End
Fiction Records, April 1992
Chart Position: 1

SHOW

Tape / Open / High / Pictures Of You / Lullaby / Just Like Heaven /
Fascination Street / A Night Like This / Trust / Doing The
Unstuck / The Walk / Let's Go To Bed / Friday I'm In Love /
Inbetween Days / From The Edge Of The Deep Green Sea /
Never Enough / Cut / End
Fiction Records, September 1993
Chart Position: 29

PARIS

The Figurehead / One Hundred Years / At Night / Play For Today /
Apart / In Your House / Lovesong / Catch / A Letter To Elise /
Dressing Up / Charlotte Sometimes / Close To Me
Fiction Records, October 1993
Chart Position: 56

LOST WISHES

Uyea Sound / Cloudberry / Off To Sleep . . . / The Three Sisters
Fiction Records, November 1994
Available on cassette only direct from Fiction Records

Video

STARING AT THE SEA
Killing An Arab / 10.15 Saturday Night / Boys Don't Cry / Jumping
  Someone Else's Train / A Forest / Play For Today / Primary /
  Other Voices / Charlotte Sometimes / The Hanging Garden /
  Let's Go To Bed / The Walk / The Lovecats / The Caterpillar /
  Inbetween Days / Close To Me / A Night Like This
April 1986

THE CURE IN ORANGE
Introduction / Shake Dog Shake / Piggy In The Mirror / Play For
  Today / A Strange Day / Primary / Kyoto Song / Charlotte
  Sometimes / Inbetween Days / The Walk / A Night Like This /
  Push / One Hundred Years / A Forest / Sinking / Close To Me /
  Let's Go To Bed / Six Different Ways / Three Imaginary Boys /
  Boys Don't Cry / Faith / Give Me It / 10.15 Saturday Night /
  Killing An Arab / Sweet Talking Guy
November 1987

PICTURE SHOW
Why Can't I Be You? (12″) / Catch / Hot Hot Hot!!! (12″) / Just Like
  Heaven / Lullaby / Fascination Street / Lovesong / Pictures Of
  You / Never Enough / Close To Me (Closer Mix)
July 1991

PLAY OUT
Day 1: London Town & Country Club 2, 17.1.91: Wendy Time /
  The Big Hand / Away / Let's Go To Bed / A Strange Day
Day 2: Wembley Arena, 19.1.91: Pictures Of You / Fascination
  Street / Lullaby / A Forest
Day 3: Tonight With Jonathan Ross, 23.1.91: Hello I Love You / Just
  Like Heaven / The Walk / Bland With An Edge / Harold And Joe
Day 4: E-Zee Hire Rehearsal Studio, 22.1.91: The Blood / The Walk
Day 5: MTV Unplugged, 24.1.91: Just Like Heaven / A Letter To
  Elise / If Only Tonight We Could Sleep / Boys Don't Cry
Day 6: London Dominion Theatre 9.2.91: Rehearsals for Brit
  Awards

Day 7: London Dominion Theatre, The Brit Awards, 16.2.91:
   Never Enough
November 1991

SHOW
Tape / Open / High / Pictures Of You / Lullaby / Just Like Heaven /
   Fascination Street / A Night Like This / Trust / Doing The
   Unstuck / The Walk / Let's Go To Bed / Friday I'm In Love /
   Inbetween Days / From The Edge Of The Deep Green Sea /
   Never Enough / Cut / End / To Wish Impossible Things /
   Primary / Boys Don't Cry / Why Can't I Be You? / A Forest
October 1993

Sources

The magazines and newspapers below have been shamelessly plundered for this book. We offer our grateful thanks to all those writers and editors who made their work available so freely.

BLITZ
Cured? – Jonh Wilde, 5/89

INTERNATIONAL MUSICIAN & RECORDING WORLD
Dave Allen: Track Record – Andrew Smith, 6/89

KEYBOARD
A Cheerful Note On Disintegration – Robert L. Doerschuk, 10/89

LIME LIZARD
The Cure – Britt Collins, 3/91
The Cure – Philip Milo, 4/92

MELODY MAKER
A Demonstration of Household Appliances – Nick Kent, 19/5/79
Primary Cure & the Picture Tour – Adam Sweeting, 2/5/81
Taking The Cure – Steve Sutherland, 13/8/83
The Glove Will Tear Us Apart – Steve Sutherland, 3/9/83
Disturbing Old Ghosts – Steve Sutherland, 1/10/83
Territorial Rites – Steve Sutherland, 15/7/89
A Midsummer Night's Dream – Steve Sutherland, 23/6/90
Visionary Chic – Steve Sutherland, 22/6/91
Pictures Of Youth – Stud Brothers, 7 & 14/3/92

Friday I'm In Chicago – Andrew Mueller, 5/9/92
Wishing Impossible Things – Simon Reynolds, 19/12/92

NEW MUSICAL EXPRESS
Days Of Wine and Poses – Paul Morley, 12/7/80
Rock Versus Greengrocery – Richard Cook, 13/8/83
Top Cat! – Mat Snow, 26/5/84
Inbetweenies – David Quantick 14/9/85
Ten Years In Lipstick And Powder – James Brown, 8 & 15/4/89
Paint Your Bandwagon – Roger Morton, 27/10/90
The Mansion Family – Andrew Collins, 18/4/92
Boozing's My Religion – Roger Morton, 12/6/93

Q
In Search Of El Dorado – Johnny Black, 7/87
Caught In The Act – Robert Sandall, 5/89
Robert, Do You Still Collect Pens Please? – Miranda Sawyer, 5/92
Who Are You Calling Laughable, Dull, Unattractive, Doleful, Po-faced, Lazy And Badly Attired? – Stuart Maconie, 7/93

RCD
I Wish – Gavin Michie, 4/92

Record Collector
The Early Years – Pat Gilbert, 7/93
The Cure – Pat Gilbert, 8/93
The Cure – Pat Gilbert, 9/93

SELECT
I'm Getting One Of My Headaches – Chris Heath, 8/91
My Little Phony – John Robb, 5/92

SOUNDS
Kill Or Cure – Dave McCullough, 27/1/79
Cure Pop For Now People – Dave McCullough, 12/5/79
Elliptical Image Games – David Hepworth, 8/9/79
Manhattan Interiors – Phil Sutcliffe, 3/5/80
Playing For Today – Simon Dwyer, 8/11/80
Progressions Of Power – John Gill, 13/6/81
Kill Or Cure – Dave Henderson, 16/7/83

SOURCES

(Sc)Avenging Angels – Bill Black, 2/6/84
Bobby Soxer – Carole Linfield, 24/8/85
Sex Rituals And Territorial Rights? 24/5/86
Impossible Dreamer – Robin Gibson, 11/7/87
The Final Score – Keith Cameron, 22/7/89
Kiss And Make Up – Sam King, 17/11/90
The Crimson Scorcher – Ethlie Ann Vare, 24/11/90

THE TIMES
Curious Case Of The Cure – Johnny Black, 26/4/89

VOX
Mixed Up Kid – Betty Page, 12/90
Making Up The Cure – Shaun Phillips, 11/92
Runaround Sioux – Steve Malins, 12/92
Putting The Boot In – Marianne Johnson, 12/93

ZIG ZAG
Beautiful Dreamer – Jonh Wilde 6/82

Index